Plundering Hell to Populate Heaven:
The Reinhard Bonnke Story

*a **DOVE Christian Book** by Ron Steele*

WITHDRAWN FROM
M.C.S. LIBRARY

D1113853

E.P.B.C. LIBRARY
Peterborough,   Ontario

Plundering Hell to Populate Heaven:

The Reinhard Bonnke Story

by Ron Steele

DOVE Christian Books
Melbourne, Florida

E.P.B.C. LIBRARY
Peterborough, Ontario

Unless otherwise indicated, all Scripture quotations are taken from the *King James Version* of the Bible. Other quotations are from *The Living Bible (TLB)*, copyright ©1971 by Tyndale House Publishers, Wheaton, Illinois, and from *The Holy Bible, New International Version (NIV)*, copyright ©1978 by the International Bible Society and used by permission of Zondervan Bible Publishers.

© 1987, 1988 **by Reinhard Bonnke Ministries**

P.O. Box 3851, Laguna Hills, CA 92654-9952

ISBN 0-88144-091-4

Production by
Publications Technologies
Eau Gallie, Florida

Printed in the United States of America

Published by
DOVE Christian Books,
P.O. Box 36-0122, Melbourne, FL 32936
Melbourne, Florida

CONTENTS

ABOUT THE AUTHOR

Ron Steele, 47, has been a professional journalist in southern Africa for 29 years.

He also has been a pastor in Lusaka, Zambia, where he gained experience as a newscaster on Zambia Television.

For the past five years, he has worked with some of the major Christian ministries in South Africa. He was associated with Reinhard Bonnke for four years, working as his public relations and publicity agent.

AUTHOR'S NOTE

This book is the welding together of two books, *Plundering Hell*, which was published in February 1984, and *Populating Heaven*, which was released in November 1986. Neither book was published in America. It was then decided to edit them and combine them into one complete story for release in the United States of America.

Assisting in this task has been Connie Blackwell of Media Consultants, who read through both books and then set about the job of merging the two titles.

The purpose of the book is not to exalt any man but to exalt the Lord Jesus Christ and to challenge Christians to walk in bold, new dimensions of faith.

In addition to Connie Blackwell's contribution, I wish to thank Reinhard Bonnke for the opportunity to write this book and for making available to me tape recordings, documents, and back issues of Revival Report magazine. Also, to the Bonnke Ministries' general manager, Peter Vandenberg, and the many members of the team: You have all contributed to this book.

Finally, the dedication of the book is to the Man Who died for me — Jesus Christ.

Ron Steele
Johannesburg, South Africa
February 1987

FOREWORD

Reinhard Bonnke is one of the most outstanding missionaries in our world today. He has a vision for Africa that is an inspiration to all who hear it, and his effectiveness in ministering to hundreds of thousands on that continent is setting an example for the entire Christian church.

It has been our pleasure at CBN to give wholehearted support both spiritually and financially to Reinhard Bonnke's work. This account of his incredible ministry will read like something out of the Book of Acts. The only difference is the magnitude of the numbers of people involved probably exceeds anything that we have known in ancient or modern history.

I commend for your reading pleasure PLUNDERING HELL TO POPULATE HEAVEN.

Pat Robertson

1

AFRICA *SHALL* BE SAVED!

I will build my church; and the gates of hell shall
not prevail against it.

Matthew 16:18

Africa has been known for years as the Dark
Continent. Today, it is also being called the Dying
Continent.

Famine and disease, including the modern-day
plague of AIDS, are torturing countless numbers of the
five hundred million people who live on the continent.

Several of the fifty-three independent nations of
the continent are in a state of civil war or some internal political upheaval.

In the past, Africa has experienced the imperial
might of Portugal, France, and Britain. Today it is a
continent free of those old empires. Imperialism has
been replaced by bloody dictatorships, one-party
political systems and other variations on democracy,
and, of course, a sinister mixture of socialism and
Godless Marxism.

Despite its savage beauty of thundering waterfalls,
surging rivers, tropical jungles, and savanna grasslands,
Africa's future is bleak, if not desperate.

Poverty and death haunt the continent, but against
this gaunt background comes a cry: "Africa shall be
saved!" Not by big business. Not by grandiose food aid
plans. Not by some political genius. No, nor by might
nor power, but by **My Spirit, saith the Lord** (Zech. 4:6).

The man proclaiming this message of hope is West German evangelist Reinhard Bonnke, who believes he has been given a divine challenge to preach the Gospel from Cape Town to Cairo, from south to north, from east to west, across the rugged continent of Africa.

Ever since he set foot on the Dark Continent, in May 1967, Reinhard has been consumed by a holy flame. Yet, when he and his pregnant wife, Anni, and seven-month-old son Freddy came down the gangplank at Durban harbor, he had little idea of the saga that was to unfold.

If he had, the 27-year-old Reinhard may well have shepherded his young family back aboard the ship and disappeared into the backwaters of northern Germany to live out the relatively sedate life of a pastor.

Reinhard Bonnke did not come to southern Africa as a novice preacher, however. He had ministered in Germany as both a pastor and evangelist before becoming a missionary.

That first day off the ship, he was wondering whether his boyhood dreams would be fulfilled. There was no denying the supernatural signposts that God had planted along the pathway on which He had set Bonnke's feet years ago as a lad in war-torn Europe.

Escape From Danger

Reinhard's father served with the Wehrmacht during World War II. The family, consisting of his mother, four brothers, a sister, and Reinhard lived in Konigsberg, capital of East Prussia. In 1945, it was a town of ruins as streams of German troops and vehicles fell back in retreat from the Eastern Front and Russian forces advanced. Russian planes constantly flew overhead bombing the retreating forces and civilians alike. Only five years old, Reinhard vividly remembers the sounds of war, such as the post office building down the road from their home receiving a direct hit.

Mrs. Bonnke, a dedicated Christian, had believed the family would be safe at home, but some German soldiers persuaded her to take the children and leave when the town seemed to have been set ablaze. It was the beginning of a nightmare journey, but also a miraculous one. That winter's night as she gathered the family together to flee, flames leaped skyward from bursting shells and burning buildings. With each child carrying a bundle of personal belongings, the mother led her precious brood out of their home and down to the main road.

Although it was a bewildering experience, Reinhard does not recall being afraid. Instead, their journey in the midst of noise and confusion seemed like some exciting adventure. As the heavily laden army vehicles trundled past, Mrs. Bonnke waved her arms, desperately trying to get one of the trucks to stop and give them a ride. At last, as the little group huddled together for comfort, a truck did stop. A voice yelled from the cab that there was only room for three, but Mrs. Bonnke ignored the voice and kept lifting children up into the back until all were in — then she squeezed in as well.

The vehicle was old, creaky, and wood-fired. As the driver jerked through the gears, they moved off down the road. Reinhard saw the brightness of flares being dropped by enemy planes through the darkness, but he was so exhausted that he fell asleep in the arms of one of the soldiers.

When morning came, everyone was cold, dirty, and hungry. Nerves were raw as Russian fighters strafed the snaking line of trucks fleeing the advancing enemy troops, and bombs gouged ugly craters in the road along their route. The roadside already was dotted with the grotesque sight of dead bodies. Night and day, the smell of death was present, and Reinhard's young mind was assaulted by the sights and smells.

When they could ride no farther on the army vehicle, the Bonnkes took to the road on foot. They trudged for several days before managing to get another ride. During this time, they survived on a few meagre slices of bread and, at night, sought shelter with others at deserted farmhouses. The escape route led across the Haff Sea and, in the late winter weather, ice was beginning to melt. The crossing was particularly treacherous with vehicles often axle deep in melting ice, a comparatively thin cover over the deep, freezing waters surging beneath. Only days after the family made it across the sea, Russian planes bombed the ice, and thousands of soldiers and civilian refugees lost their lives in the icy waters.

Bedraggled and weary but still together, the mother and six children eventually reached the port of Danzig (Gdansk today), which was filled with refugees from the immediate battle zones. The only way of escape was across the Baltic Sea. In Danzig, however, there was family — an aunt and Mrs. Bonnke's devout Christian mother. With thousands of others, they waited prayerfully for a ship on which to embark for Denmark and safety. Once they wistfully watched a ship, the Gustlov, steam out of the harbor crammed with eight thousand women and children. Two days later, however, they heard that the ship had struck a mine, and only two hundred people survived.

Air raids increased, and the Russian forces were drawing nearer when the Bonnkes finally got a berth on an ancient coal steamer. Before they sailed, the mother and grandmother gathered them together and read Isaiah 43:16: **Thus saith the Lord, which maketh a way in the sea, and a path in the mighty waters.** This Scripture gave them all great comfort, and Reinhard still remembers how moved his mother and grandmother were and how they knelt in prayer and committed themselves and the children to the Lord.

The morning they were to board the ship, the gangway was a seething mass of human bodies, pressing and shoving to get aboard. Air raid sirens shrieked warnings, and they wondered if they would ever actually get aboard. Eventually, however, they arrived safely below deck, and the ship steamed sluggishly out into the Baltic on the start of another ordeal and another example of the providence of God. They were attacked several times from the air as the ship plowed through the rough wind-ruffled waves. One incident is still etched plainly in Reinhard's mind. He had just clambered up a rusty ladder to get to the sanitary facilities on deck, and he watched in awe as a Russian plane wreathed in flames plunged into the sea, a victim of the steamer's anti-aircraft guns.

Conditions were cramped with everyone herded together beneath the decks. There was no privacy, of course, and people were sick. Their moans and groans filled the air day and night. The food, even for those well enough to eat, was poor. There were very few smiles and little to ease the tension. Then, one afternoon, things got worse: the ship struck a mine. It shuddered and pitched violently as if the steel-plated sides were being ripped apart. The vessel then developed a heavy list to one side, and fear gripped the refugees who clung to one another almost hopelessly in the darkness and dampness below decks.

Mrs. Bonnke held onto the Word of God that she had read before leaving Danzig and comforted the children. Suddenly, the ship began to right itself, and some of the crew told them that pumps were beginning to cope with the flood of water pouring in below them in the hold. More than forty years later, Reinhard can still close his eyes, cast his mind back to that voyage, and hear those pumps clattering away night and day during the rest of the trip. To those on board, the clattering pumps made the most heavenly symphony as, it seemed miraculously, the ship stayed afloat. Before long, a cheer of relief went up from the crew and the tear-stained travelers as the coast of Denmark came into view. They were safe at last — the Lord had truly *made a path* in the waters.

The Bonnke family was safe, but the children had to wait three and one-half years before being reunited with their father. He also was a Christian, having been converted after being healed of tuberculosis as a young soldier. Later, he began attending the local church and married the organist, who became Reinhard's mother. By 1945, the elder Bonnke was an officer. Shortly after the family reached Denmark, he arrived in Danzig with other senior military men. There was a lone mine-sweeper in the harbor with a limited number of available births. When the other men learned that he was married with six children, they made him take one of the remaining places. The ship left harbor and, a few days later, was intercepted by a British naval vessel. The Germans on board were put in a British prisoner of war camp at Kiel.

Meanwhile, Mrs. Bonnke and the children lived in Denmark as refugees until being returned to a war-ravaged land now occupied by the Western allies. When Bonnke was released, the family was reunited at Gluckstadt late in 1948. Although he had not seen his father in almost four years, Reinhard recognized him instantly and remembers running into his outstretched arms. By that time, his father had been called to preach and was ready to become a full-time pastor. The setting and preparation for Reinhard's spiritual development was now ready, and God was about to move in a direct and personal way in his life.

Preaching to the Trees

Reinhard's mother led him to the Lord at nine years of age, a few months after the family was reunited. Then, to make it "proper," he responded to an altar call in the local church to make a public commitment. As a child, he was aware of spiritual things. In spite of getting into the same kind of mischief other boys his age did, he remained basically a serious-minded child. Jesus was the center of his life, and even sports held little attraction for him. Jesus was his boyhood hero, and remains his hero as an adult. He did have an ear for music and learned to play the piano and accordion, but that talent was used to worship and serve the Lord. There was never a place for worldly distractions in his life. His favorite "game" was to go out into a nearby woods and preach to the trees.

"A friend and I would go off where nobody could see us or hear us, and we would preach out our hearts to the trees. My friend was a much better preacher than I was, and I used to wonder whether I would ever be good enough a speaker to stand behind a pulpit," Reinhard says.

The childhood friend, however, has never preached a real sermon, while flesh and blood audiences of thousands have come to hear the shy and diffident boy who used to preach to trees. The thin alto voice that challenged the tall pines of northern Germany to repentance now shouts "Hallelujah" in a rasping baritone in churches from England to South America and from Canada to Australia. In small, dimly lit halls, chrome and glass auditoriums, tents, and even the naked bush of Africa, the grown-up Reinhard has sounded the good news of the Gospel.

His parents really did not understand the depth of his spiritual devotion as a child. They lived a frugal life in the countryside, governed by the traditionally strict German discipline and the restraints of the holiness teachings of the Pentecostal church to which they belonged, but prayer meetings were not obligatory.

Reinhard recalls, "I was not allowed to go to mid-week prayer meetings, but I really wanted to go. I wanted to be there, but when my mother saw me weeping because I could not go, she relented. It was the first time she had ever heard of a little boy crying because he could not go to church!"

During one of those mid-week prayer meetings, a woman said God had given her a vision. In it she

16

saw a little boy breaking bread before thousands of black people. She turned to Reinhard standing next to his father and announced, "This is the little boy I saw in the vision." He was ten years old at the time. This was the first of many dramatic supernatural encounters that were to punctuate the adventurous path that would lead him to one day challenge Satan head-on over the wind-swept veldt of southern Africa.

In addition to devouring the Bible, Reinhard read stories of famous missionaries and heard visiting missionaries speak at his father's church. He became full of the desire to go to the mission field by the time he was eleven. To his parents, these were just the daydreams of an overly serious little boy, but he refused to be discouraged. Some of his friends used to tease him as "the little missionary," but he cherished and held onto the desire in his heart. Then, as a teenager, the Holy Spirit gave him a confirmation of his own in a dream to add to the vision related by the woman at the prayer meeting. He dreamed of a map of Africa with only the name of one city on it — Johannesburg.

"I must confess that my knowledge of the geography of Africa was not too good then, and when I awoke, it bothered me that the name of the city was so far south. I was sure the real place was nearer central Africa. I immediately got out a map of Africa and found that the One who designed the planet knew His geography better than I did. There was Johannesburg exactly where I saw it in my dream," Reinhard relates.

The dream, though, did not bring any dramatic change or any direction. Life went on as usual and, at nineteen, Reinhard was admitted to the Bible College of Wales, eager to equip himself for the mission field.

Again, his parents and friends at the local church did not understand his decision to attend the non-Pentecostal, conservative, evangelical Bible college which he had heard about from a visiting preacher. Nor did the elders of the church where he meant to attend college understand any better. This German youth who wanted to attend college could not speak English! However, the immediate witness in his spirit when the college was mentioned was enough assurance that this was the place where the Lord wanted him to study.

Despite his youth, however, Reinhard was sure that he knew God's will for his life. He respected his elders but refused to allow them to discourage him or to swerve him from his set course anymore than he had the other children when he preached to the trees. That certainty on knowing the will of God and the determination to stick to a settled course have become characteristics readily recognizable to those with whom he has dealt over the years. Some people have thought his steely determination was disguised stubbornness, especially when he began to carve out a ministry under the African sun. His faith, however, is fearless in the face of any Goliath or any criticism.

So he packed his suitcase, placing his well-worn Bible in between his shirts, and headed across the English Channel. Looked at in the natural, the situation did seem odd. Why would God send a German youth to a Bible college in Wales in order to send him as a missionary to Africa? Through such instances as this in his early life, Reinhard has learned to trust God and not question Him. There were particular influences and experiences in that place that would equip him specifically for the future God had planned, although there were German colleges just as good which would have been nearer home and less trouble to attend. Perhaps it was simply trust and faith that he was learning by having to depend on God in alien circumstances, but he knew early that obedience always pays even if one never understands the reason on this earth.

2
LESSONS IN FAITH

The first three months at college were agony. He took it for granted that he would have to write all his examinations in English, not realizing that he could have gotten permission to have written all or part of them in German. He set himself to learn English, however, and after only three months was preaching on weekend assignments without an interpreter, an amazing accomplishment.

He listened with great concentration to the lecturers and at night would go through his lessons by candlelight with a dictionary at his side. It was not easy, but there were some compensations. The college rules were all printed in English so he inadvertently broke every one of them at one time or another. Once he received a severe reprimand for filling his bath up to the brim, which was forbidden in a big notice on the bathroom door. As he relaxed in the steaming bath, water was pouring through the overflow pipe into the courtyard above the main entrance to the men's dormitory! Another advantage to speaking a foreign language was being able to pray in tongues without offending fellow students or lecturers. They thought he was just praying in German.

He soon found his decision to attend the college confirmed by the things he learned about the Word of God. One of the first things he discovered was that the staff all "lived by faith." None of them drew a salary. They received room and board but had to trust God for anything more. For example, if the cook needed new equipment in the kitchen, she did not put through a requisition to the college office. Instead, she prayed for what she needed and trusted God to supply. To Reinhard's surprise, the principle seemed to work, and everyone was surviving. As the staff members prayed for their needs and received the answers, they used a statement that soon became a catch phrase for the students: "I have been delivered."

Once as the students were gathered for a prayer meeting, the college president came in and announced that the equivalent of several thousand dollars in American money was needed by the end of the week to pay the bill for coal. He said, "I just want you to pray. We make no financial appeals." That is a lot of money today and meant a lot more in 1960, and Reinhard thought to himself: "Now let's see what happens." At the end of the week, the president again attended the prayer meeting and triumphantly proclaimed to the students: "Praise God, we've been delivered!" That incident focused the young student's attention on prayer and faith. From that moment, he earnestly began to pray, "Lord I want to be a man of faith if You are prepared to trust me."

Once the seed of faith was planted in his spirit, he immediately decided to put it to the test. Up until then, Reinhard had been well taken care of financially by his parents and members of his home church in Germany. He received packages of goodies and supplies from home as well as pocket money and funds to pay his college fees. Now he began to seek God for this "real" faith. The message he received from the Lord was clear: "If you really want to become a man of faith, give away all the money you have. Give it to a missionary who passes through here, and then you will see what I will do."

Reinhard eagerly accepted the challenge, but tried to keep back just a few dollars "in case of an emergency." This brought a swift comment from the Lord: "You see? You don't give Me a chance to do a miracle. How can I do a miracle if you take care of yourself? You haven't given Me a chance." It was a solemn moment as the quiet voice of the Holy Spirit echoed in Reinhard's heart. That day, he saw the deep-seated, self-help program that is in the human heart. He saw how people ingeniously look after themselves and, by so doing, cut out God, not giving Him half a chance to prove His power.

So he gave away all his money and progressively learned that a man of faith gains rich rewards, not just for himself, but for the Kingdom of God — although there may have been a few occasions when he felt that a tide of doubt would drown him. He set out to experience faith-living for himself, and an opportunity to test his faith came soon.

He was given an assignment to speak at a young people's meeting a bus ride from the school. He had money for the round trip fare for one person, but he wanted to take along a friend to help. So he went to the friend, Tuinis, a Dutch student, and asked him to go along. The two students boarded the bus in high spirits having spent all the money both had on two one-way tickets. The meeting was a success, and the young people listened eagerly to the Bible stories. It was a beautiful day. The sea was calm, and children played happily as people strolled leisurely along the beach.

Reinhard really did not have time to enjoy the holiday atmosphere, however. He was busy praying:

"Lord, we need our return fare. I am testing you now for the first time to see whether Your Word is true. I gave all my money away, and I had enough money for a round-trip ticket if I had come by myself. But I wanted to test You for the first time."

As he stood with his Dutch friend on the shore, they spotted a local pastor whom they knew.

Immediately, Reinhard thought, "Praise God, here comes our deliverance. If God can speak to anyone here, it surely must be this pastor because he is a man of God."

The boys greeted the minister enthusiastically and their faith soared as they were invited to join him for a cup of tea in a nearby restaurant overlooking the beach. As they sat together sipping tea, exchanging stories, and listening to some of the pastor's experiences, Reinhard's spirit was sending out an SOS over and over: "Lord, just enough for bus fare. Speak to this man. Just enough for bus fare!" Still trying to help the Lord along, he finally spoke up and said, "Our bus is coming soon. We must not sit here too long." So the minister called for the waitress and paid the bill. The youths could not help but notice that inside his wallet was enough for bus fare several times over.

"Well, it has been nice running into you boys. Keep up the studies," the man said, and they all shook hands. That was it. No money. Reinhard looked glumly at his friend, and the two dragged their feet as they walked to the bus stop. Black clouds of doubt began to hover over Reinhard. He wanted so much to see God provide, but now . . . . As his mind wrestled with the situation, suddenly he became aware of someone running behind them. They turned and saw an elderly lady, handbag swinging on her arm. A bit out of breath, she almost knocked them down as she reached them.

"Boys," she said, fumbling in her bag for her purse, "I liked your little message so much. Here, take this," and she held out to them two English coins that were twice as much as they needed to catch the bus. Reinhard and his friend smiled broadly at each other. "Praise God. Lord, You are faithful," they said. Rushing off rejoicing, they bought their tickets still marveling at God's goodness. Surely those coins had been minted in Heaven!

That was his first genuine answer to prayer. "Deliverance" had not come from the source which he expected, and right there he learned a major lesson in living by faith: Never count on what may seem to be the obvious thing in the natural. Also, he learned never to look to people with money and think because they have it they will supply your financial needs. The Lord's work is still supported in the main by "the widow's mite."

His studies continued and his English improved — he knew that because now he could read the rules! The more than sixty students constantly were inspired by the example of the staff. The teachers were not simply interested in filling students' minds with knowledge of the Bible, they were concerned as well with shaping the characters of the young men. Part of that meant helping the students deal with the "self" aspects of the soul. Reinhard's missionary zeal grew, and the faith life enchanted him. He soon came to realize that for faith to grow, it has to be exercised;

otherwise, it will shrivel up. One cannot stay at the bus-fare level all of one's life.

One day while praying, God spoke clearly into his spirit to return to Germany during the next school holiday. Here was a second real challenge to his faith. He had no money at all, but went to a travel agent and booked passage to Germany. A few days before he was to leave, the agent called and asked him to come in and pick up his ticket. He still did not have a penny to his name. Stalling the agent off, Reinhard told him, "I will come in time. Don't worry."

With the deadline nearing, Reinhard spent much time on his knees. "Lord, you told me to give all my money away. Now You are telling me to go to Germany. You have to supply my need. I am not telling anyone about it."

The days passed, and the day before departure, he was once again on his knees. "Lord, you only have one more chance. Tomorrow before 9 a.m. I must find the money in the mail box. That is Your last chance. I see no other way. Please, Lord Jesus!"

The next morning, Reinhard could hardly keep still. He rushed through breakfast and paced restlessly up and down the corridors and through the beautiful Italian gardens that surrounded the college buildings. His whole being was focused on one thing: the money for the ticket. At 9 a.m., he ran to the mail box. Yes, there was a letter addressed to him. His heart beat faster as he ripped it open — this must be it. His hands were shaking slightly as he pulled at the contents of the letter expecting a check to fall out. What a disappointment! The letter was junk mail, a routine advertisement. He felt as though a bucket of ice water had been poured over his head and stood staring blankly at the worthless piece of paper in his hand.

Something inside of him seemed to be saying, "Hang on." Trying to hide his disappointment, he walked quickly back to his room. There was only one resort — pray again. As he knelt beside his bed, his Dutch friend Tuinis joined him. While they were praying, the travel agent called again. In an urgent voice, he said, "Mr. Bonnke, when are you coming to collect your ticket? Your train leaves at 1 p.m." Reinhard took a deep breath and said as calmly as he could, "Don't worry. I will come and get it in time."

The words, "Don't worry," echoed in his mind. His ticket was booked, everything was ready to go — but he did not have a penny to his name. He could hardly believe the reality of the situation as he walked away from the telephone and went back to praying. Again, he cried, "Lord, You told me to give my money away. You told me to return to Germany. Now I am testing You. You promised, but time is running out."

The minutes passed by . . . 10:30, then 11 a.m. came. Reinhard and his friend went off to one of the classrooms where they could shout to God. Maybe praying louder would get an answer. As they began to pray out loud, the words of a chorus suddenly came to Reinhard's lips, one the students often sang: "There is nothing too hard for Thee." The two young men began to sing that song. When they sang the last verse, Reinhard experienced something that, even today, he finds difficult to explain. That little mustard seed of faith to which he had clung seemed to grow and grow. It was as though he had entered a new dimension. In his spirit was a calm, divine assurance that all was well.

With the words to the last verse still lingering in the air of the classroom, he jumped to his feet and exclaimed, "The money is there!" His bewildered friend looked up and said, "Where?" His answer was, "I don't know, but I know it is there." They left the room and raced across the garden toward the front of the college. As they rounded a big hedge, a man came running toward them. He was tall and breathing heavily, but he looked straight at Reinhard and asked, "How much money do you need?" Reinhard stared at him for a moment. This was it! "God knows the amount," he answered, "I'm not telling you." The man dug into his pockets and stuffed a handful of money into his hands. "There," he said, and before Reinhard could speak, the man turned around and left.

He counted the money, and it was the exact amount needed for the fare. He grabbed his suitcase out of his room and ran for the bus. In town, he charged into the travel office, paid for his ticket, and raced for the railroad station where his train would be leaving in fifteen minutes. He must have looked like a marathon runner at the end of a race. The train was actually moving as he flung open a door and flopped into the nearest seat. He was exhausted physically, but his spirit was rejoicing. Now he knew beyond any doubt that God answered prayer. If He would provide for an unknown German Bible student in Great Britain, then He would provide for him when he went to Africa.

After two years, Reinhard successfully passed his examinations, and with Bible and diploma under his arm, was ready to win the world for Jesus, or more explicitly, to win Africa for Jesus. But the gateway to Africa was barred at that time because he was considered too young, so God restrained his zeal and led him into the evangelistic work in Germany. Here he got his first taste of crusade work and of preaching in tents. Standing under the canvas canopies preaching the Gospel to fellow Germans, he had little idea that tents would someday become the trademark of his own ministry, one of the world's most anointed and dynamic Gospel outreaches.

When he moved to Flensburg, also in northern Germany, and pioneered a church with the help of a friend, it seemed that the dream of going to Africa was fading. Especially when he met the young lady who was to become his wife, and the Bonnkes settled down to a modest church routine. In 1966, a son, Freddie, was born to Reinhard and Anni.

Yet Africa tugged at his heart. He would not lose the vision, but obviously God would not let him go yet. It was a period of apprenticeship and growing in grace and experience. After eight years, the doors began to swing wide and circumstance made it possible for him to go to Africa as a missionary.

When he announced to his thriving congregation that he was going to Africa, they were dismayed. Some thought it was bravado. The majority of his friends begged and pleaded for him to stay, but there was no way anything or anyone was going to keep him from going to Africa. At last, after eight years, Africa was in his sight. He could almost see the grass huts and feel the burning sun. No soppy sentiment was going to dissuade him from fulfilling his life's calling. Africa was waiting.

3
GOD'S FAITHFULNESS

His first year in southern Africa was almost a disaster. He worked in Ermelo where the Bonnke's second child, a daughter named Gabi, was born. Reinhard had come to Africa with his own ideas about how a missionary should operate. One of the things he cherished was freedom, and he did not take kindly to the shackles of mission boards. He had to grit his teeth firmly, however, and tighten his belt. He still does not talk much about that first year on the mission field. He learned to submit to his superiors, although he disagreed with some of their methods. They felt he needed to be eased gently into the new conditions and needed time to learn and observe the many strange traditions and ways of life in Africa. While his desire was to get out and preach to the African people.

He desperately wanted to fly from the cage of circumstances in which he felt trapped, and he began to eye the independent nation of Swaziland. Then he got the opportunity to visit Maseru, the capital of the mountain kingdom of Lesotho. What he saw there touched him. Once the British Protectorate of Basutuland, Lesotho was a poor, landlocked country. The people lived off the land, and there was very little industrialization. Hundreds of thousands of young Basuto men still travel each year to work in the gold mines of South Africa, bringing home good pay checks and luxury items. "There was a spirit of helplessness about the place," he recalls. After returning from Maseru, there was a restlessness in his spirit. He knew that he had to make a move — or perish. He could not stay any longer at that time in South Africa. But where to go? He wanted desperately to please God, not to stray from His sovereign will. He wanted to stay within the bounds of the plan that God had drawn for his life.

The next morning, while reading his Bible, a passage in Judges seemed to leap up at his eyes. Not only did it seem to indicate Lesotho, but it also promised the blessing to accomplish the job that God wanted him to do in that poor, neglected country. Arrangements were made with his mission board, and he got a green light from his superiors who obviously had faith in this enthusiastic German missionary with such a burning zeal to preach the Gospel to the African people. Often he had felt like Samson shorn of his hair, but now he was going to be given the opportunity to flex his muscles. After a year of standing patiently in the wings, the call had come. He was ready to step out onto the stage of the rugged, mountain country of Lesotho.

Blanket of Death

The Bonnkes did not move to Lesotho immediately because they already were living just across the border at Ladybrand, a small farming town in the Orange Free State. Once their third child, Susi, was born in May 1969, however, Reinhard and Anni moved to Maseru to live among the people with whom they were working.

From the beginning of their marriage, Anni has been the perfect homemaker and mother, spending her time caring for and rearing the children. Absolutely devoted to her husband, she is extremely shy of publicity and dislikes the limelight. Seldom does she ever make any public speeches. But her husband is the first to admit that he could not have accomplished God's purpose in his life as readily without her support and assistance. Truly, her reward will be gained in Heaven.

The move to Maseru gave Reinhard his freedom. For the next six years, he worked tirelessly at evangelising the nation. Those were hard, tough years. The children were growing up, and his son Freddy began attending the local school.

Looking back, he would call that time the "lean time of the ministry." Despite all his efforts in preaching from village to village, building a fine church in Maseru, starting a Bible correspondence course that reached thousands all over Africa, he was still not satisfied. That is the dynamo that hums within his spirit. He is an achiever and a perfectionist. His heart is always striving for a closer relationship with God. He deliberately wants to delve into God's limitless supply.

Although he may not say it, Reinhard also loves a challenge. At heart, he is an adventurer, a man who will dare anything for God — no matter how difficult the task. While other missionaries might have boasted of success, he was looking at the Lesotho scene with critical eyes. He examined the work and himself and came to a staggering conclusion: it was not enough. That missionary urge in his heart was not satisfied. There had to be another challenge, something bigger to tackle. Only God knew what it was, but Reinhard was willing to risk all by leaving Lesotho and heading for Johannesburg.

Somewhere in his spirit, that map of Africa with Johannesburg still glowed. If that dream had been from God, he must go to Johannesburg, the city of gold — but before that, he had a close brush with death.

Carelessly, he had drunk some unboiled water. On a blazing hot day with hardly a cloud in the sky, he had been driving along the twisting, dusty mountain roads visiting local pastors. His throat was parched when he arrived at the small village of Kolonyama, and he felt as though he had trekked across the Sahara. The offer of a cool drink of water was like stumbling into a green-fringed oasis, so he gulped it down.

That night, he fell sick with what he thought was a bout of dysentery. By the next morning, he was desperately ill and lay in the bed exhausted, slipping into fits of delirium. His wife prayed at his bedside, and the message went out to his fellow pastors to pray. As the fever raged, he got weaker and weaker. Unable to eat, he was fast losing contact with what was going on around him.

On the third day, he experienced a strange vision. His eyes were wide open, and he saw a black blanket floating down toward him apparently about to cover him up. Instinctively, he knew the blanket was death. He found that he could see through the blanket. On the other side was a face — the face of Jesus. Despite his delirious condition, a soothing comfort came over him as he gazed at the Lord's face. Then something even stranger happened. He was suddenly conscious of someone praying, someone agonizing in soul, crying out and pleading with God, begging and pleading for his life. He knew the voice. It was that of Eliese Kohler, a dear, loyal, and devoted member of his father's church in Germany.

As he listened to her praying, the blanket began to fade away. Reinhard recalls that he slipped off into a quiet, restful sleep. The hot fever that seared his body subsided. The crisis was over, and Reinhard would survive to preach many more sermons. He was many weeks recovering, but he wrote to his father and asked him to contact Mrs. Kohler and ask her what had happened on the day he had seen the "death blanket." His father's reply confirmed what he believed. The prayer warrior had risen early and been urged by the Holy Spirit to pray for Reinhard. As she prayed, the burden so intensified that she realized a fight for his life was going on. She spent virtually the entire day praying for him. To Reinhard, it underlined once again the mighty power of prayer. A woman had prayed in Germany thousands of miles away, and God had acted because of the faithfulness and obedience of one woman. Since that time, Reinhard has experienced the power of prayer in his own life on many occasions.

Chariot of Fire

Two further incidents of note occurred in Lesotho. Both were linked and, once again, meant the opening of Heaven's curtain for God to supernaturally intervene in his ministry.

One incident still makes him blush to this day because it involves a financial deal that went wrong. He was taken for a ride and could have paid dearly for it in hard cash. Across the hall from his offices in Maseru was a business selling furniture from catalogs. Some of the African pastors came and asked Reinhard to help them buy some furniture. "Survival wages" was about the best description of his own salary in those days, but the pastors kept pressuring him each time they visited.

"I was really on the spot," he says. "I knew the poor conditions in which those pastors lived. For the most part, old, discarded items made up the bulk of their household furnishings. So I prayed, 'Lord Jesus, You said we should not close our hearts. I am going to do something I have never done before. I am going to borrow money and lend it to these pastors, my dear brothers.' "

So the pastors went over into the other office and ordered some furniture. When they told him how much they had gotten for the amount of money they had, he became suspicious. He asked the salesman how he could sell so cheaply. Was the furniture stolen? The man assured him everything was in order, so contracts were signed and money paid in advance. Four weeks later, the deal exploded. The furniture was being bought on hire-purchase agreements across the border in South Africa, and the sale of the goods in Lesotho was illegal.

Through a phone call from one of the pastors, he learned that the salesman was going to skip across the border. "Please stop him. Get a lawyer. Otherwise, we are going to lose everything," pleaded the pastor. As Reinhard put down the telephone, his spirits were low. He wondered what lawyer he could get. Then, slowly, he bowed his head, and prayed, "Lord Jesus, You are my lawyer. I put this case in Your hands."

The next morning, a pastor was waiting when he arrived at the office and wanted to know if he had contacted a lawyer.

"Yes," replied Reinhard.

"Which one?"

"The best in town."

After a pause, the pastor asked, "Who is that?"

"Jesus," smiled Reinhard.

He recalls that the pastor's face did not show much emotion, but says, "I felt he was disappointed. My case was resting with Jesus, however."

The furniture man did skip the country, and the pastors never got their furniture — but the devil was not able to steal the money from Reinhard. Two weeks later, Reinhard was invited to speak at some special meetings. He had not told anyone about his unfortunate loss, feeling honestly ashamed about the incident. After one of the services, a man came up to him and pressed an envelope into his hand with a gift for "his own personal use." When he opened it, there was the exact amount he had lost on the furniture transaction. He was able to pay off the loan he had taken. "The wonderful thing about it," he laughs, "is that my Lawyer charges no fees!"

The second incident also involved finances, but came from a very different angle. It is best told in his own words:

"I was driving through the flat, almost treeless Orange Free State. The Bible correspondence course had been going for five years with an enrollment of fifty thousand. It was a costly business to keep going, and I was always scratching around for extra finances.

"To save expenses, I bought envelopes in bulk — one hundred thousand at a time. I had to wait until I had saved enough cash before I ordered them. As my well-worn Mercedes diesel-engined car pounded along that day, I was reflecting on that unhappy furniture deal in which I had become involved. 'Lord,' I prayed, 'there is one thing I will never be able to understand. If I had borrowed that money to enrich myself, I could understand why You allowed me to fall into that pit. But You know better than anyone else that I borrowed that money to help the poorest of the poor. I did it for Your Word's sake. I did it for my brother's sake. Lord, I cannot understand why you allowed this to happen.'

"What happened next is hard to describe. Suddenly, Jesus was tangibly in that old car. It was as if it had become a flaming chariot filled with the glory and presence of God. Tears gushed out of my eyes, and I thought I was in Heaven. The spiritual fulfillment which I experienced at that moment cannot be put into words. I was no longer conscious of steering the vehicle or of the passing scenery. I felt as though I was being wrapped up in God's glory and being posted to Heaven. The thoughts of the furniture money disappeared. Then I heard a voice say: 'The flour in the box shall not diminish and the oil in the cruse shall not become less.'

"I knew what the words meant. I had two mission accounts at the bank. I said, 'All right, Lord, of my two accounts, one is the box and one is the cruse. My duty is to pour them out, and Your job is to fill them up.' That was in 1970, and I have never managed to get into the red with the work God has sent me to do in Africa. I have sometimes overspent, only to find that the amount was covered by some anonymous deposit."

There is no doubt that he has pushed hard to empty the barrel! Sometimes his bookkeeper has thrown up his hands in despair when accounts have fluttered on his desk like confetti, but somehow they all get paid. Not that Reinhard is reckless with finances, and neither is he extravagant. Because of his strong determination to accomplish the divine task given him, however, he sometimes strains the purse strings.

In later years, when the Big Tent eventually came into production, it proved a tremendous financial drain on the entire organization of his ministry. The men working on the tent demanded more and more equipment, and he could not turn a deaf ear. The Big Tent got preferential treatment which led to some frustration as other outreach work had to take a back seat at times. Reinhard's coolness in the midst of a cash crisis, however, must surely be traced back to that supernatural encounter on a lonely stretch of road.

A Modern Elijah-Baal Encounter

Now followed an event that totally reshaped his ministry. It was almost like having Moses' rod slapped into his hand or the mantle of Elijah slide over his back. Although it looked like a disaster, the incident signaled the beginning of a new ministry. At the time, however, he almost visualised himself being stoned at the city gates!

In many ways in the early 1970s, Reinhard was just another missionary toiling away under the scorching African sun. People got saved, people got baptized, but ministry was one long continuous struggle. People kept saying that Lesotho was "a difficult place for the Gospel." He says, "I agreed with them heartily, so I kept repeating that. Little did I realize that I was snaring myself with those words. I prayed earnestly for a major breakthrough but became even more convinced that 'this place is too difficult.' When fifty people were at a service, I thought the Great Outpouring had begun!"

Deep inside, however, he longed for something bigger and greater, something to bring resounding praise to God, something that would shake people out of their lethargy and demonstrate that Jesus is alive, something that would cause men and women to come to the Savior in large numbers. With this in mind, he invited a well-known evangelist with an anointed healing ministry to preach at two services.

Reinhard and his associates were wildly enthusiastic. The printing press was running furiously to get out handbills and posters telling about cripples walking and the blind being made to see. They even managed to get some time on the local radio station. His faith was higher than Mt. Zion as the time for the crusade drew near. The services were the talk of the town and the church was packed for the first one. Surely this was the breakthrough for which he had been praying! Now the superstitious minds of those who trusted in witchcraft would see what the Lord Jesus could do.

He stood on the platform that night looking out at what seemed to be a sea of faces, more people than he had ever seen in the building before. He was touched as the lame limped down the aisle looking for a place to sit and some twisted human forms dragged themselves along on all fours to get into the church. The sight of those mangled, twisted limbs moved his heart. Oh, to see these people healed by the power of God was the cry of his heart as the African voices were lifted in hymns.

The meeting began. The visiting evangelist preached a good sermon, but the atmosphere was not right. Very little happened. In fact, midway through the evening, the evangelist turned to Reinhard and urged him to close the service. Reinhard was flabbergasted. "I can't do that," he said. "These people want you to pray for them."

"No. Close the meeting," the evangelist argued.

Reinhard's mind was in turmoil as hundreds of eyes stared at the two preachers waiting and hoping.

"All right, I will close the meeting, but you must promise to pray for them tomorrow morning." The evangelist agreed and the meeting was closed.

As he turned off the lights and locked the church doors, he was very sad. Everything seemed right for a revival. One look at the faces of the people would have told anyone that. As he went to bed, a little gust of apprehension stirred his heart. Surely things would be better tomorrow, he thought, pushing fear away. Sunday morning dawned. He arose, washed, and shaved, then went to pick up the evangelist. To his amazement, he found the man in his safari suit with his suitcase packed about to climb into a waiting car.

"What is happening?"

"I am going home," the man replied.

"No, you can't do that. You dare not. I have just come from the church. It is full. There are even more people than were here last night. You cannot go." There was a note of despair in Reinhard's voice. How could this man desert him with the church full of people waiting for him to pray for them?

The evangelist turned, looked him right in the eye and said, "The Holy Spirit told me I must go."

Reinhard checked himself. That was a different situation. "If the Holy Spirit told you, then you have no option. You must go. You dare not disobey. God bless you, and goodbye."

He watched the evangelist drive off, then climbed back into his own car very upset, and cried out to God. "I am not a big-name preacher. I am just one of Your little men, a missionary; but, now I will preach at this meeting, and You will do the miracles."

In utter desperation, his old car slid to a stop at the church in a cloud of dust. He would have to preach. There was nothing else to do. Muttering a prayer under his breath, he called the African pastors together and told them what had happened. As gloom settled over them, he ignored the protests. "I am going to preach, and God is going to do the miracles," he told them with a boldness that surprised even himself.

Bible firmly clasped in his hand, he strode up onto the platform knowing what was going through the minds of each person watching him: "Where is the great man of God?" Looking straight at the audience, he told them the evangelist had gone — then he held his breath. What would they do? There was a shuffling as two men got up from the front row and walked out. Would that be the signal for a mass exodus? No. As the men pushed their way through the crowd, others began elbowing their way toward the front, eager to gain a better vantage point. The rest of the audience just sat, waiting.

As he began to preach, an anointing of the Holy Spirit fell upon the people. Never before had he experienced the power of God with such intensity. The interpreter broke down in the middle of the message and sank to the floor with tears pouring from his eyes because of the holy presence of God. As Reinhard paused, waiting for the interpreter to regain his composure, he "heard" words that almost left him speechless: "My Words in your mouth are just as powerful as My Words in My own mouth." His senses reeled, and then he heard the sentence repeated. He recalls that, like a movie film, he "saw" the power of the Word of God. God spoke, and it happened. Jesus had told His disciples to speak to the sycamine tree, and it would wind up in the sea. (Luke 17:6.)

"I suddenly realized," he says, "that the power is not in the mouth — the power is in the Word."

In the meantime, the interpreter had regained his feet. Reinhard continued his message, then again the voice of the Holy Spirit prompted him: "Call those who are completely blind, and speak the Word of authority." Hardly daring to believe what he was "hearing" but certainly not daring to disobey, he called out to the totally blind to stand up. About six people stood up.

As the blind people stood next to their seats, he began to have second thoughts. The devil dropped into his mind this thought, "What if nothing happens?" Then, he says, "I whispered under my breath, 'I am going to do what Jesus told me to do.'"

All eyes were on the missionary as the jabber of the people ceased, and he knew this was the moment of truth — for him as well as for the congregation. He spoke to the blind people and said, "Now I am going to speak with the authority of God, and you are going to see a white man standing before you. Your eyes are going to open."

41

It could have been a modern-day Mt. Carmel duel, with the servant of God poised to call down fire on the sacrifice to Baal as the cultic priests looked on. Surrounded as he was by Africans who were firm believers in the power of the supernatural as manifested in witchcraft, Reinhard knew that it was not *his* reputation at stake. Taking a deep breath, he shouted, "In the name of Jesus, blind eyes open!" The power of his voice jolted even those on stage as if a flaming bolt of lightning had flashed through the church. His voice was still echoing from the bare brick walls when a woman shrieked. What she screamed shattered the composure of the congregation: "I can see! I can see!"

The woman, who had been totally blind for four years, leaped toward Reinhard. Almost out of control, she grabbed people around her demonstrating that she could now see. The congregation began to shout, and the church erupted in bedlam. The woman fought and pushed her way through the mass to get to the microphone. "Whether you believe it or not, I can see," she said. "Give me something to read. I can see again."

The congregation sounded more like a crowd at a football game as cheers erupted throughout the building. A young woman with a crippled child tried to get to the front but could not for the crowd, so she handed the boy over her head to be passed on until he was thrust into Reinhard's outstretched arms. As the child lay helpless, Reinhard prayed and then sensed a surge of God's power through the little body. The child's legs began to vibrate. Amazed at what he was seeing, the evangelist put the little boy down on the platform, and it was like putting a wind-up toy down. He stood for a moment, then began to run with his crippled legs straightening out before everyone's eyes. He ran to the right and then to the left. The screams and shouts of the people sounded like torrents of mighty waters.

The meeting continued for several hours with countless people being prayed for by Reinhard and his co-pastors. The church was filled with singing and praise. The people of Maseru knew that morning that Jesus is alive beyond any shadow of a doubt. When the service ended, and the last few people left, one man remained. Reinhard walked quietly into a darkened corner of the now-empty church, bowed his head, and with folded hands prayed, "Thank You, Holy Spirit for sending the big evangelist away. Thank You, because now nobody can say it was him. Now everyone will say it was Jesus Who did the miracles. This is how I want to serve You. This is how I want to work with You."

4
A MILLION SOULS

During the last quarter of 1974, Reinhard visited South Africa several times for discussions with the executives of Apostolic Faith Mission (AFM), the denomination with which he has been associated since coming to Africa, about moving to Johannesburg. The Lord was shaking him loose from the roots he had put down in Lesotho.

Once, he heard the Lord speak clearly into his heart: "Do you want me to give you a million dollars?" What a wonderful thought. He naively believed at that moment that he could win the world if he had that much cash. Then something stirred deep in his soul, and ignoring passersby, he raised his hands in the air with tears in his eyes and cried, "No, Lord. Don't give me a million dollars; give me a million souls. A million souls plucked out of Hell's jaws. A million souls for Heaven." Out of this encounter came Reinhard's now famous war cry: "Let's plunder Hell and populate Heaven."

If he were to get those million souls for the Lord, then he knew they had to move. So in October 1974, the Bonnkes bought the house which was to be their home for about ten years. The house was in Witfield, a suburb of Boksburg (about twelve miles east of Johannesburg), and they moved in just before Christmas. As another indication of the Lord's providence, Anni says, "There was only one house unsold in the new development, and of them all, that was the only one that I would have wanted." Another

indication they were on the right path was that the Holy
Spirit had indicated their headquarters should be near
Jan Smuts Airport, South Africa's international
terminal, and Witfield is less than ten minutes from
the airport.

Never a man to go easy on himself, Reinhard often
operates dangerously near his physical limit. Shortly
after the move, Anni began to notice an unusual
lethargy about her husband. His usual zest for life was
gone. Finally, he had to confess that he was a sick man
— hard to accept for someone who preached that Christians were not only saved from sin but delivered from
sickness and disease. He had seen miracles of healing
with his own eyes. Now his prayers did not seem to
be bringing any results in his own life.

"I was very sick, and didn't think I was going to
make it. I went to doctors, but nothing helped. I cried
to God, 'Lord, what are you doing? What is your plan?'
One afternoon a thirst for prayer came over me, and
I was barely on my knees when I saw a most wonderful vision. I saw the Son of God stand in front of me
in full armor, like a general. His armor was shining like
the sun and burning like fire. It was a tremendous sight,
and I realized that the Lord of Hosts had come to me.
I threw myself at His feet and laughed and cried for
I do not know how long. When I got up, I was perfectly
healed," Reinhard relates.

A Momentous Year

That was early in 1975, which was going to prove
a momentous year in his life. He was to initiate an
extraordinary Gospel outreach into the sprawling black
township of Soweto, next to Johannesburg, and was to

launch Christ for All Nations (CFAN) with the ministry headquarters located within a couple of miles of his home. He established his own ministry because the AFM Home Mission Board would not always back some of his projects, and he realized that he would need an outside source of funds. While in Lesotho, he had gained private support for some of his own projects, and to avoid any financial queries and to ensure his integrity and reputation, he kept separate accounts — his own and the denomination funding account. The ministry name had actually been registered in 1972, but it was three years later that CFAN, the name by which his ministry is popularly known in Africa, was seen in banner-size letters over a crusade for the first time.

Botswana Breakthrough

Reinhard had always been acutely aware of the importance of radio to missions and had started broadcasting while in Lesotho. Response from the local programs and others aired in Ghana, Zambia, and Swaziland had been encouraging. Tens of thousands of people wrote in to take his Bible correspondence courses and to tell of accepting Jesus as their Savior. One man was sitting in his car with a hose running from the exhaust pipe trying to commit suicide when he turned on the radio to get some music to cheer him into eternity. Instead of music, he heard Reinhard's voice challenging him to repent and accept the Savior. The man did just that, quickly dismantling his suicide apparatus and driving home to tell his family of his new Friend, Jesus. (The courses have since been discontinued. Reinhard has no regularly scheduled radio or television programs, but the ministry does produce audio and video cassettes.)

So in 1975, he turned his attention to Botswana, another landlocked neighbor of South Africa, also bordered by Namibia, Zambia, and Zimbabwe. A desolate country, Botswana consists mostly of the harsh Kalahari Desert and is famous for its bushmen, the little people who survive by the most primitive means. The country does have a radio station, however, which is beamed into many neighboring countries. Reinhard flew into the capital of Gaborone on his trip to buy airtime on this station. As the plane made its approach to land, he looked down at the monotonous brown countryside and caught a glimpse of green — the Botswana National Sports Stadium, which meant nothing to him then. Sports did not interest him, but little did he realize that the sports stadiums built to celebrate independence were to become an arena for the preaching of the Gospel.

Strolling along the sidewalk in the blazing morning sun, he found himself going past the National Sports Stadium. To use his own words, suddenly he was "rooted to the ground" when the voice of the Holy Spirit spoke clearly: "I want you to preach My Word there." He quickly responded, "Lord, You have said it, and I am going to do it. I believe You."

Inside, his spirit surged like a giant ocean wave trapped in a rocky cove. He sensed this was not just a fleeting wave of joy, but something different. This could be why God called him out of Lesotho. Soon he was in discussions with a local pastor, and negotiations for radio time were no longer a priority.

The pastor was excited over a city-wide crusade, but became cool when Reinhard mentioned hiring the stadium. Obvious doubt showed on the man's face. Perhaps he thought the German brother was suffering from a touch of the sun! Reinhard repeated his request and asked that the city hall be hired also in order to begin the campaign. The pastor scratched his head and politely told Reinhard that he was obviously unaware of the local situation. He said, "Why, I only get forty people out to a Sunday morning service, and you are talking about hiring the stadium! Surely, brother . . . ."

Displaying what may have appeared to be presumption but in reality was faith, Reinhard did not even allow the man to finish the sentence. His mind was made up based on the Word from the Holy Spirit. "Hire the biggest hall in town," he said, "also make arrangements to get the use of the stadium, and I will be back in thirty days with a team." He flew back to Johannesburg to organize a crusade team with a heart full of expectancy.

A Dream of Mass Evangelism Fulfilled

By April 1975, the crusade had been publicized widely, and posters had been put up all over town. The local pastor had worked feverishly to herd up as many people as possible, bringing them in cars to the city hall. Reinhard and the first CFAN team, consisting of a small group of workers and a big lovable middle-aged Zulu pastor as co-evangelist, arrived for opening night to find one hundred people in the hall which seated eight hundred — and the stadium seated ten thousand!

The local pastor, however, was thrilled at the "crowd." He warned Reinhard not to expect any larger

crowds after the first night because his entire congregation of forty persons was there, and there just were not
any more people he could bring. Reinhard's faith had
been maturing over the years, and he refused to be
stampeded into panic. He knew the devil was an
accomplished bluffer, but that God holds the winning
cards. Still, it took courage that night to face the
audience and tell his co-workers that God was going
to fill the hall. He preached and his co-evangelist prayed
for the sick, and things began to happen.

People began to leap to their feet exclaiming,
"Something happened to me. I am healed!" Others,
touched by the power of God, collapsed and slumped
to the floor. This continued night after night. The team
was thrilled by the miracles but puzzled by the new
(to them) and strange phenomena of people falling
down under the power of God. When people began
to ask what was happening, Reinhard gave this
explanation: "The Bible speaks about signs and
wonders. It is not a wonder when somebody collapses,
but surely it is a sign — a sign of God's presence."

By the end of the first week, the eight-hundred seat
hall was overflowing with close to two thousand people
with some sitting in others' laps, some sitting on the
floor, and some in the windows. A sardine can would
have looked like a palatial ballroom compared to that
hall. People were being drawn in by the talk of miracles
and healings, just as the news of miracles and healings
had spread across the sunny fields of Galilee almost
two thousand years before. Jesus was walking through
Gaborone, and the people were flocking to meet Him.

When Reinhard first entered the sports stadium
hired by the no-longer doubting local pastor, it was

almost like a dream in spite of his faith. He had nursed the dream of crusade evangelism and big crowds with mighty miracles since his youth. This was what he had longed to see but had not dared to share for fear people would think he was boasting. Now thousands filed in to hear the Gospel, and many university students streamed to the front when the altar call was given. Before the end of the crusade, there was another spiritual surprise which came like an explosion.

The Baptism of the Holy Spirit

One night, the Holy Spirit urged, "Pray for the people to receive the baptism in the Holy Spirit." So he got one of his African workers to give a lecture on the Holy Spirit baptism. The man did his best, but it was a confused teaching. He left out what to Reinhard was the most important point — speaking in tongues. Reinhard was about to get up and correct this omission when he was checked. The Holy Spirit said, "Just keep on sitting. Stay where you are." Although frustrated in the natural, he remained seated and waited obediently on the Lord's next move.

When those wishing the baptism were asked down to the front, about a thousand people responded. The moment they raised their hands and stood, it was as if a bomb had exploded. Within seconds, all those standing had been flattened in disorganized piles of people, all of whom were shouting and praising God in a new language. Reinhard gaped amazed at the holy disorder. Never before had he witnessed such a thing. These people knew nothing about speaking in tongues, yet here they were shouting praise to God in other languages. Tears filled his eyes as the phrase from the

Book of Joel surfaced in his mind: **My Spirit upon all flesh . . . My Spirit upon all flesh** (Joel 2:28). As he stood there under the starry night sky with a symphony of heavenly languages rising into the still air, he prayed, "Let Your Spirit fall on all flesh in the whole world."

As the crusade ended and the team left Botswana, Reinhard made a decision and a commitment before God: "Lord, I have tasted honey. I will never be satisfied with syrup any more. No substitute will do. It is this or nothing." The Lord answered, "I will be with you. Go on."

Beyond any doubt, God had given him a vision for Africa. Looking at the giant continent with its size, its complexities, and its heathenism was enough to daunt the faith of any mortal, and he knew that only the power of the Holy Spirit could meet this challenge. Anything less would produce failure.

The pattern for his ministry was now clear, and the dream was beginning to be a reality. He would become acknowledged by all as an evangelist, not simply a missionary. He had tasted the first fruits of mass evangelism. At heart, however, he remains a humble man just as much at home in a small country church. In addition to the big crusades, which he loves because that is his main calling from God, he speaks at churches and breakfast sessions.

Soweto Township: Lazarus at the Rich Man's Door

With his great capacity for work, Reinhard had initiated an unusual outreach into Soweto at the same time that he was preparing for the mass evangelism breakthrough in Botswana. Sprawling along the out-skirts of Johannesburg, the name of Soweto is now known in many parts of the world because of the social unrest and riots that arose there. Soweto's world recognition for such sad reasons did not occur, however, until eighteen months after he received the charge from God to take the Gospel there. To spiritual eyes, it is quite obvious that the devil began to stir up trouble to try to stop a revival in Africa; although, of course, the awful conditions of life in the township should have been addressed by governing authorities and churches long before.

There was no electricity in 1975 in Soweto. The streets were dust and stone or mud and slush when it rained. Huge craters marked the roads that snaked in between dingy, grey buildings. More than one and a half million people now live in the depressing town. Rural residents come to find work in the "City of Gold" — Johannesburg — resulting in overcrowded housing. At times, there may be fifteen people living in a one-bedroom block house. There are not enough jobs for all, so there is high unemployment. The crime rate is high, and illegal bars or taverns, called shebeens, are found everywhere. Drug traders move freely through the back lanes, and murderers, muggers, and rapists stalk the streets after sundown.

The township is also home, however, to hundreds of thousands of honest people who travel into sur-rounding towns to work. Despite the awful social problems, the crime, the still powerful influence of witch doctors, Soweto is not totally a den of thieves. It has a place in God's plan of salvation for mankind. The Lord spoke to Reinhard about the township shortly after he had been dramatically healed. The Word he received was very clear:

"Soweto is like the poor man Lazarus at the door of the rich man, Johannesburg. You dare not ignore him. You have got to do something for him."

It seemed obvious to Reinhard that God wanted to save many thousands, because in the mire of Soweto there were hearts crying out for God's mercy. To evangelize the "poor man," he adapted a bicycle strategy which he had used in Maseru. By faith, he got together a bicycle brigade of dedicated witnesses for the Lord, loaded them up with Bibles, hymn books, and Christian literature. In Maseru, they had gone out into the lonely mountain villages with their materials and their testimonies. Some of them even took to horseback in order to reach remote villages high up in the rugged ranges of the Malutis Mountains.

His instructions from the Holy Spirit were to buy one hundred bicycles, each fitted with a large carrier on the front and to send Gospel witnesses house to house with literature and personal testimonies. His bicycle brigade also was to pray for the sick. He told no one about the plan for Soweto except his wife. Soon, however, people began calling or stopping by the office — some complete strangers — asking, "Do you need a bicycle for the mission work?" Soon he had fifteen of the special bicycles. Struck by how quickly everything was coming together, he remarked to Anni, "It seems as though God is pushing us from behind. He is pushing us as if He were in a hurry." There was an urgency in the task the Lord had given him that he had no idea what was about.

At that point, he began to share his goal of reaching Soweto with others. Usually, he is very reluctant to make appeals for money. His approach is to share the vision from God, then challenge people to share in the ministry by praying and giving whatever they can afford. His fundamental belief has always been that God is the Provider. In 1975, he was still ultra cautious about appeals. So he was thrilled when a man came up after a church meeting in Johannesburg and asked, "How much money do you still need for your project?" When told that another eighty-five bicycles were needed, the man promised, "I'll give the money for all the bicycles."

With a song in his heart, he visited the cycle factory, negotiated a good price, and signed the contract. But when he phoned the sponsor to tell him of the price, the man said, "I have made a mistake. I am sorry. I cannot give you anything." Reinhard wondered whether his ears were playing tricks on him, or whether the man was just a joker. He was in deadly earnest, however, and Reinhard was left holding a signed contract for eighty-five bicycles and not a penny to pay for them. His spirit of joy braked to an abrupt halt.

Instead of becoming angry at the errant sponsor or trying to bully him into keeping the promise, Reinhard allowed him to withdraw his offer. "I told him I wanted to remain friends, but that if he could not trust God, then he should trust me to trust God!" He sets himself not to make enemies and never to hold a grudge.

As usual in such cases, however, he did not receive much help from some friends who took the role of "Job's comforters." They began to criticize and doubt his vision for Soweto, and to make such comments as "We always knew it was a mistake," or "This was too

big a bite. We knew you were going to choke to death."
One even asked him why he had to have a hundred
bicycles, "Is that a magical figure?" To which, Bonnke
replied, "No, it is not. It is God's figure, and that is all
there is to it."

Refusing to be swayed by critics or doubters, he
continued to plan for the Soweto outreach and within
the next four weeks, the required finances for the
bicycles flowed into the ministry. After he visited his
homeland for a brief preaching tour, German Christians
became the largest contributors to the project.

So with military-type planning, Operation Soweto
was mounted. A huge map dominated the ministry
offices as territory was assigned to workers. Pastor
Johan Venter of the AFM was a key figure in organizing and running this exciting new evangelistic project.
The bicycle evangelists did a tremendous job, working
long hours each day. Within eight months, the goal had
been reached. Every house had been covered.

It was June 1976, and the last evangelist had hardly
pedaled back into headquarters when the news came
that Soweto was aflame. Large-scale rioting had broken
out and police had been called in. The army was on
standby, and cars and buses were being stoned and
burned. Lawlessness reigned for several weeks.
Thousands of workers stayed home, afraid to venture
out into the streets where vicious fighting was going
on between police and rioters. Many died. At night,
the sky towards the southwest of Johannesburg was a
red glow as burning and pillaging continued.

Now Reinhard knew why God had been in such
a hurry and why one hundred bicycles had been
needed. Otherwise, the project would not have been

completed in time, and some of those people would never have had an opportunity to hear about Jesus. Certainly, after the riots, evangelists were not able to move through the township easily and in safety. The Soweto episode made a lasting impression on his commitment and on his walk with the Lord.

"What if I had not obeyed? What if I had compromised on the number of bicycles? I determined more than ever to walk a strict path of obedience, never questioning God's wisdom," he says.

Another lesson he learned was that God never has to rely on just one man to finance His projects. An incident that helped bolster his faith was the visit of an elderly lady the day after the sponsor had reneged on his promise. She gave Reinhard money for one bicycle and said, "Every day I will think of that man on my bicycle going from door to door. I will be praying for that man every day." Then the evangelist realized that God not only wanted bicycles and witnesses, he wanted a prayer partner to back up each of the men in the field. Gold and silver does not impress God as much as people to pray for His work. The evangelists in the field needed that intercession to move into the tough township and take the Word house to house.

One of a thousand incidents that could be told of snatching someone from the gates of Hell in Soweto occurred when police entered a home searching for a man accused of murder, but stopped at the bedroom door to see him down on his knees giving his heart to the Lord. They stood back and waited for the evangelist to finish before taking the man off for trial.

The bicycle evangelism campaign was not the end of the Bonnke ministry's Soweto connection. Reinhard would return there twice, and the second time would involve the opening of the world's biggest Gospel tent. In 1976, however, that part of the plan of God was still hidden from view.

5

A "NURSE" FOR
THE GREAT PHYSICIAN

Three other crusades — one in South Africa, one in Namibia, and one in Swaziland — and the purchase of the land for CFAN headquarters were high points of 1976. One day a man from Reinhard's home suburb of Witfield told him about a property for sale. The man said, "There is a Scotsman living in the old white house on the plot near to the railway line, and he wants to sell it to me for a nursery school, but I am not too keen on it. Would you like to have a look?"

Quick to sense a divine opportunity, Reinhard jumped into his car and drove off along a bumpy, dusty track. The old farmhouse, formerly white but now a sickly yellow, did not look very impressive. It was surrounded by tall grass and a glorious crop of weeds — certainly no Garden of Eden. But from the moment the soles of his feet touched the ground there, Reinhard "knew" it was to be his headquarters. As usual, when beginning any new project, there were no funds, and pretty soon he found there were ten bureaucratic reasons why authorities would not allow the deal to get off the ground. Reinhard's comment, "The reasons are in our favor," did not make sense to his colleagues. He knew, however, that the land would be his and told the CFAN board of directors to close the deal. "In the name of Jesus," he said, "I will pay the full amount on the day of transfer."

Three months later, he sat down and wrote out a check for the full amount. The red tape had been worked through, and the funds had come in. When the board first saw the land, one of the members quipped, "Maybe Reinhard is going farming." Looking at the overgrown acreage, he wondered himself. Now it belonged to the ministry, but what was God going to do with it?

Over the next three years, what God was going to do with it gradually took shape. On May 4, 1978, the office complex was officially dedicated by Dr. F. P. Moller, AFM president, and Pastor J. W. Gillingham, who served on the CFAN board for more than eight years.

A Mission at the Gates of Hell

The first crusade of 1976 illustrated what the famous English preacher Charles Haddon Spurgeon meant when he once wrote, "I don't want a church in the vale. Give me a mission at the gates of hell."

Held at Port Elizabeth in New Brighton, South Africa, CFAN had hired the four-thousand seat Centenary Hall for the two-week crusade. One night, the Lord moved so strongly that the sermon was never finished. Suddenly, people began streaming to the front weeping like children. A shower of cigarettes, knives and other instruments, witchcraft fetishes, and stolen articles landed on the platform as people came under conviction and began throwing away those articles of sin.

One young man, who was only about twenty years old but whose face was a network of knife scars, came up one night and gave the pastor a homemade vicious-looking knife, saying, "Here, pastor, take it. I have decided to give my heart to Jesus."

Flooded by a wave of compassion, Reinhard leaned over and whispered, "Thank you, Lord. What no policeman could ever do has just been done by the Holy Spirit."

During the second crusade of the year, in Namibia, Reinhard prayed for a man suffering from cancer in one ear and with no eardrum in the other. When he had finished asking God to heal the one ear and perform a creative miracle in the other, the man began to jump up and down: He could hear with the ear that had no eardrum. At first, even Reinhard was incredulous, then he thought that God Who created us must have all the spare parts we will ever need.

That concept sums up much of his approach to healing. Not wasting any time debating the theological pros and cons, he just sails along praying for the sick. If they get healed, he rejoices with them. If they do not, he calmly rests the case in the care of God's sovereign will and great mercy.

At one point in his ministry, he says that questions about healing concerned him, but then the Lord showed him that he was only the "nurse." Jesus is the Great Physician. He says:

"The more I thought about it, the happier I became. I realized that it is the physician's place to diagnose the disease and prescribe the medicine. All I have to do is follow behind the doctor and carry the medicine. It just remains for me to administer the dosage as prescribed — and then it works. **By whose stripes ye were healed** (1 Pet. 2:24), the prescription says, and **they shall lay hands on the sick, and they**

shall recover (Mark 16:18). So all I am is a nurse, and I am very happy to be one for Jesus."

He witnessed two other remarkable healings that year, both involving people suffering from terminal cancer.

The first case was a woman who had heard a cassette tape of one of his sermons in which he related miracles performed through his ministry and that of a co-worker, Michael Kolisang. She also read often from a book about Habakkuk 3:19 which had been brought to her in the hospital by her husband.

The Lord God is my strength, and he will make my feet like hind's feet, and he will make me to walk upon mine high places.

She felt that verse had some special meaning for her. But she was sent home from the hospital to die. Then a friend said that God had told him to bring Pastor Bonnke to pray for her.

Although he was involved in a conference and felt he could not take the time, when the man called and made the request, Reinhard heard the Holy Spirit say in his heart, "I am sending you." Michael Kolisang, an early associate in Maseru who had joined the Bonnke ministry, arrived in Witfield the morning of the visit, so Reinhard took him along. When they met the man who had called and who was to guide them to the woman's house, the man gave Reinhard's associate a perplexed look and said, "Look, I have nothing against black people, pastor. He is a dear brother. But we are going to visit Dutch Reformed people, and I don't think they would like a black man to come into the house."

Reinhard replied, "Don't worry. Mike understands South Africa. He can wait in the car while I pray for the woman."

As they drove along the Johannesburg-Pretoria highway, the racial question soon faded from his mind as he prayed about the woman they were to visit. What Scripture could he give her? Suddenly, verses from the Old Testament flashed into his mind:

> **Although the fig tree shall not blossom, neither shall fruit be in the vines; the labour of the olive shall fail, and the fields shall yield no meat; the flock shall be cut off from the fold, and there shall be no herd in the stalls:**
>
> **Yet I will rejoice in the Lord, I will joy in the God of my salvation.**
>
> Habakkuk 3:17,18

As they neared the outskirts of Pretoria, Reinhard wrestled with the verses. "Lord, I can't give her that scripture. It sounds as if she is going to die. Everything goes wrong in those verses. No, Lord!"

But the Holy Spirit indicated once again, "Give her that scripture."

As they drew up in front of the home, he asked his African friend to remain in the car. He was still uncomfortable about the verses he was to give the woman, yet he was determined to be obedient.

The woman's face, a mask of death, lit up as he walked into the bedroom, and she told him of listening to the cassette and praying that she might meet him and Pastor Kolisang. At the mention of his friend's name, Reinhard exclaimed, "Just a minute, my sister. I will call Kolisang. He is right here with me now and waiting outside in the car!" As Kolisang entered, it was obvious there was no racial prejudice in that house.

Reinhard opened the Bible and read the passage from Habakkuk. As he read, the sick woman began to weep and to tell them of the book she had been reading in the hospital on that very chapter. She handed him the book with almost every sentence underlined.

"Well, I am convinced that God is here to do a miracle," Reinhard told her.

The little group gathered around the bed, and as they laid hands on the patient, the room was filled with the glory of God. She whispered, "I have a vision. I see myself standing under a mighty waterfall." She looked stronger by the time they finished praying, apparently wonderfully healed in an instant. Less than a week later, she went through three days of intensive testing at the Cancer Research Institute, and all the tests and X-rays proved negative. The doctors were astonished at no trace of cancer being found.

There is a sequel: God not only healed Mrs. Dinnie Viljoen but gave her a ministry to the Afrikaans-speaking people of the Dutch Reformed Church. She criss-crossed the nation for a year, telling her story and seeing countless women won to the Lord and set free from religious bondage. On the anniversary of her healing, she arranged for the use of a nearby Presbyterian church and Reinhard spoke to some four hundred people. As he drove off that afternoon waving good-bye, Mrs. Viljoen was radiantly happy. It was the last time he was to see her.

He flew to West Germany the next day for a preaching tour, and while he was gone she died. He believes firmly that if he had been in South Africa and able to pray and counsel with her, she would not have died.

"Of course," he says, "I can only speculate about that. I do know that her life was extended by God for one wonderful year. During those twelve months, she accomplished more for the Lord than she had in all the previous years of her life."

The second case of praying for a terminally ill cancer patient came later in 1976, when he visited a man in the cancer ward of Johannesburg General Hospital. Unable to find a parking place, he told his wife to keep circling the hospital until he came out. The Word from the Lord for this person was Psalm 118:17: You **shall not die, but live, and declare the works of the Lord.** After reading the Bible and praying for the man, who seemed to relax, Reinhard hurried out to catch Anni, still patiently driving around and around the hospital.

A year later, he learned the rest of the story when a strapping young man walked into CFAN headquarters. He said, "Pastor Bonnke, do you remember me?" That is always an embarrassing question for a traveling evangelist who sees and prays for thousands of people each year. He studied the man's face for a few moments, but had to confess that he could not remember him at all. With tears in his eyes, the young man said:

"I am Kruger, the man with leukemia whom you visited in Johannesburg. All those other men from that ward are dead and buried. I came here to tell you my story. When you left that afternoon, I knew the power of God had struck at the cause of my disease. I told a nurse to get my clothes, that Jesus had healed me and I was going home. She was not impressed and thought I was losing my mind. I told her to call the doctors and get my clothes. I was leaving.

"When the doctors came, they did not want to let me out, but I stubbornly insisted. They said my healing was impossible. I said it was possible. Finally they agreed, on the condition that I sign a form absolving them of any responsibility if I died. I agreed, because I knew I was not going to die. I left the ward with a medicine chest of four hundred cortisone tablets which they insisted I carry along. I was to take forty a day. To satisfy them and get away, I took the medicine along, but once I got home, I threw it all in the trash can.

"I began to get better and regain my strength. When I went back to the hospital, the doctors were amazed. They examined me thoroughly but could find no trace of leukemia. I am perfectly well and do not even suffer from the slightest headache. I am the picture of health, thanks to Jesus," he concluded.

Plan Like a Millionaire

The final big crusade of 1976 was held in Swaziland in two different locations. That particular campaign had three circumstances that causes it to stand out in the memory of the Bonnke ministry: There was tremendous demonic opposition, there was an opportunity to hold a special meeting for the nation's royal household, and there was extremely bad weather.

From the time the crusade ministry began, Reinhard had been at the mercy of the weather. He saw that the only way to draw consistently large crowds was to provide weatherproof conditions. The only answer was a tent. He had made appeals all through 1976 for finances for a five-thousand-seat tent. They were using a smaller tent with protection for some eight hundred people when the rain pelted down that afternoon in Swaziland. The tent had been pitched in a gently sloping, basin-like area, and torrents of water came rushing down into the low-lying ground. Reinhard watched helplessly as cripples struggled and splashed to drag themselves onto higher ground.

"It broke my heart to see those sick and crippled people lie there in all that water, unable to move," he recalls, and quickly he cried, "My God, give us a roof over our heads."

Like a flash, the answer came back to his spirit, "Trust Me for a tent that will seat ten thousand." As he looked at the swirling water and the soaked and wretched people standing in the driving rain, he answered, "I trust You." That private little prayer meeting in the middle of a thunderstorm on an open field would bear much fruit. God would one day give him a tent so huge, that when he stood under its immense roof, he could hardly believe that men could have built such a thing. At that time, however, his immediate vision was for a tent to seat ten thousand.

Back in Johannesburg, he became weak in the knees when he found how much the tent would cost. Actually, most people doubted whether such a tent was possible. Certainly, there was no one in South Africa who could build a ten-thousand-seat tent. The necessary money amounted to six figures to have such a tent built overseas, to buy trucks to transport the tent and a powerful generator, and to hire more personnel. Just looking at the needed amount written on paper made him feel CFAN had been operating up to then with small change!

While pondering the plans, God spoke words that ring loud in his spirit to this day: "Don't plan with that which is in your own pockets. Plan with that which is in My pocket." Never slow to grasp revelation,

Reinhard felt of the few copper coins in his own pocket and caught a vision of God's full pocket. He prayed, "Lord, if You will allow me to plan with what is in Your pocket, then I will plan like a millionaire."

Signs and Wonders Continue in 1977

During 1977, he continued to hold crusades, to acquire vehicles and equipment, and to pray for the larger tent. Miracles and healings continued as the CFAN teams began to move out across Africa. The crippled walked, the blind began to see, and the deaf to hear everywhere the crusades were held. One deaf woman was healed when he preached on forgiveness, and she became able to forgive her husband for his mistreatment of her. Another man, Reinhard's host during a crusade, had five wives (permitted by African custom) and a lame leg. After being prayed for, he began to jump up and down on the previously bad leg, and shouted, "Look at me. I can kick the dog again!" After he had calmed down, however, he sent buses to pick up all of his relatives in the district to bring them in for a service. In the same district, a group of police came to the host's house and asked for prayer for salvation.

Of the crusades that year, the two at Giyani and at Sibasa, stand out. Giyani is a remote rural area in the northeast, bordering Mozambique. The nearest town of any size was more than ninety miles to the south. The meetings were to be held in a school hall, and the only publicity was the distribution of hand-bills. What happened, however, was the best advertising possible, and it did not cost a cent. The miracles of healing attracted more than a thousand people to the four-hundred-seat auditorium by the third night. The school principal, however, pointed out that the large crowds were making the grounds — to put it politely — rather unsanitary and unhygienic. He suggested they move to the fairgrounds some five miles away.

Although not sure that people would continue to come to the services — many already were walking long miles — the crusade was moved. There did not seem to be any alternative. The crowds continued, however, and the miracles kept happening. A clerk in the local post office told Reinhard one day that he had been a drunkard who tormented his wife and had never set foot inside a church. One night in a dream, two men in snow white garments told him, "Go to the school. There you will be shown the way of life." So he had attended the services and was born again.

As the crusade closed, Reinhard drove back to the school to thank the principal, who greeted him warmly and said:

"Pastor Bonnke, how do you manage to do what you do? I have been traveling this area many years. I know these people, but everything has changed. The whole area is different. My church has had a hospital and a mission in the district for twenty years, and you have accomplished in seven days what we have been unable to do in all that time. Normally, in such large meetings, people make heroes of the evangelists. But the people are not talking about you or Pastor Kolisang. They are talking about Jesus."

Tears came into the evangelist's eyes, and he thought that was one of the finest compliments he had ever received. Everyone's comments were not favorable, however. When a picture of the evangelist and his co-workers standing with a huge heap of crutches collected during the Giyani crusade was sent to Germany, some refused to believe the evidence. A few people from home had been openly critical of his work in Africa all along and doubted the claims of healings and miracles. They were not convinced by the photographs. In fact, they started an absurd rumor that the pile of walking sticks and crutches left behind after the meetings was "typical of African people who were absent-minded." It was hard not to resent those comments, but Reinhard later was able to answer, "Blessed is the cripple who can forget his crutches!"

Altar Call, Not Protocol

The Sibasa crusade was the real high point of 1977, and the crowds that came fully justified the decision to buy a giant tent. Located in Vendaland, in the far northeastern corner of the Republic of South Africa, the area is hemmed in by the famous Kruger National Game Park on the east and by a buffer zone separating them from Zimbabwe on the north. When the Bonnke ministry first applied for permits for a four-week crusade, the answer was an emphatic no. To make matters worse, the evangelist came down with a bout of flu.

One night, he woke up for no apparent reason, but all he saw in large, beautiful lights was the word, SIBASA. "Lord, this is confirmation," he whispered, "although we have been turned down, we will still go."

As soon as he was able, Reinhard personally visited the officials concerned and found the man he was to see was a Christian. A permit was issued, but for only ten days. A newcomer to the team, Adam Mtsweni, who was in charge of the music ministry, said, "Never mind, God created the world in six days. He can save Vendaland in seven days." Leading the singing a couple of weeks later in Sibasa stadium, Mtsweni could almost believe his words were coming true.

August in that area is usually dry and cool, so they did not have to worry about rain — they thought. The first day, however, it began to rain and did not stop. About two hundred people came out anyway. The main stand had only a small covering over it, with an unreliable generator and three floodlights providing lighting. As a precaution, Reinhard took a flashlight to the pulpit to help read from the Bible. Not only was it wet, but a chilling wind whipped across the vast, open stadium. Standing in front of his soaked audience, he wondered how they could sit so still. His own teeth were chattering and his arms and legs shivered in the unseasonably icy cold weather.

Worse was to come. The generator died, and the lights went off. As the generator usually died at least twice during a service, Reinhard took his flashlight down to those at the bottom of the stands trying to restart the generator. As he missed his footing in the dark and did a cartwheel, landing in a muddy pool of water, he found himself thanking the Lord for the darkness that kept the audience from seeing the speaker in such undignified circumstances! But he continued the service and people were healed.

The wet and the cold continued the next day. He searched the town for hot water bottles for the team, but none were to be found. Sibasa generally enjoys warm tropical weather all year round. So they put on extra socks and every shirt and top they could get over their heads. Attendance the second night amazingly doubled, and again there were notable healings. The third night the rain had stopped, and attendance doubled again. On the seventh night, some thirty thousand people swelled the stadium to capacity. Still there were problems: the public address system broke down and they had to preach through bullhorns, but the blessings continued to flow.

One afternoon while praying alone in his travel trailer, Reinhard received a clear, precise instruction from the Lord, "Go and buy a beautiful gift for the President of Vendaland."

There was nothing suitable in Sibasa, so he drove fifty miles to the nearest town and shopped until he found an attractive vase and had it gift-wrapped. He still did not know how he was going to get to see the President. As he arrived back in Sibasa, however, one of the team came running out with a message: The President of Vendaland wanted to see him at 4 p.m.

Reinhard and some of the team put on their best suits and, with his Bible under one arm, the gift under the other, and someone else carrying an accordion, he hurried off to keep this divinely appointed meeting. The President's cabinet members and their wives were at the country's "White House" when the evangelist's group was ushered into a splendid lounge where about thirty people were waiting.

President Mphephu shook hands and said, "Pastor Bonnke, I am sorry for the problems you have encountered. I have heard that God has blessed my nation through you and your team, and I have called you because I also would like to hear what God has to say to us."

Grasping the opportunity of reaching the leaders of the government, Reinhard launched into a typical Gospel sermon as if he were preaching to fifty thousand people. When he finished, for a moment he wondered what to do. He could not leave the message hanging in mid-air, but did protocol permit an old-fashioned altar call?

As that thought flashed through his mind, the Holy Spirit said, "Altar call, no protocol!"

Solemnly facing his VIP audience, he asked them to bow their hearts and pray. Then he asked any who wanted to give their hearts and lives to Jesus to raise their hands. As he glanced around at the men and women in the luxurious room, a hand went up — it was that of the President! Then came the Minister of the Interior, and others followed. Once the President led the way, "protocol" probably dictated that the others come to Jesus also. Shouts of "hallelujah" and "praise the Lord" filled the room as salvation came to the leaders of a nation.

The meetings in the stadium reached a tremendous climax with some forty thousand people attending the final service. At the closing service, Reinhard looked out over the sea of faces and suddenly remembered the scene back in that little prayer meeting when he was eleven. The woman had said she saw a little boy breaking bread before a multitude of black people, and here he was, twenty-six years later, breaking the Bread of Life before these people. The tears welled up in his eyes, and he turned aside to weep quietly as he whispered, "How great Thou art."

As 1977 came to a close, news came that the new Gospel tent would be ready and in use during the next year.

6
FAITH FRIGHTENS SATAN

There was an extra buoyancy in the spirits of the CFAN team as they set off for the first crusade of 1978. They made quite a stir arriving in the Far Northern Transvaal with the fleet of trucks and other vehicles hauling the equipment and with the travel trailers in which the team lives on the road. There was even more excitement when the new tent was raised. It was larger than a normal circus tent, larger than anyone had ever seen before. It could seat ten thousand people, but only by packing them onto tiny narrow benches. This was done on many occasions, but even then the crowds overflowed and stood several rows deep around the outside.

For the next five years, that yellow tent criss-crossed southern Africa and was set up for services as far north as Zambia. It became the embodiment of Reinhard Bonnke's extraordinary mission to the continent. First, however, there was a severe test.

The first crusade that year was a wonderful success, giving a new confidence to everyone. The second crusade, a return visit to Vendaland, was a different matter.

Instead of Sibasa in Vendaland, the 1978 crusade was in a place called Njelele, under the shadow of a sinister, brooding mountain. The new yellow tent, when first pitched, looked quite regal in its rural setting. Within a few days, however, the pride and joy of CFAN stood in the middle of a grey, wet, and desolate scene with mud-splattered sides. Part of the roof was torn and hanging in shreds.

The tent resembled a battle-scarred ship, listing heavily and about to plunge to a watery grave, as it rocked and swayed violently in the wind. Water cascaded down the sides like rapids, and around the iron tent pegs, the crew looked in despair at the giant mud pools being stirred up. Disaster could strike at any moment. Inside, the glow of the generator-charged light bulbs gave some warmth and comfort to the forlorn scene.

Reinhard bravely attempted to preach a sermon to the few hundred people who had come out in the raging storm to hear the Gospel. They seemed oblivious to the pounding rain and the danger above them, but he had barely said amen after the closing prayer when tentmaster Eugene Wurslin came stamping up the ramp to the platform. Hair plastered to his rain-soaked face, he blurted out:

"Close the meeting. It is urgent that we evacuate the tent. The pegs cannot hold any longer, and when they go, seven tons of steel and cables are going to come crashing down on the audience. It could collapse at any moment."

Even as he dismissed the crowd, the crew began to take down the tent. In between rain squalls, the wind seemed to breathe horrendous gusts from the direction of Njelele mountain — the ancestral home of departed spirits, according to local legend. When the team arrived, they had been warned about evil spirits that haunted the mountain which was held to be very sacred by the local inhabitants. A local pastor told them:

"Some time ago, a missionary came here and put a tent right where you have put yours. Before he was able to preach one sermon, a fearsome wind came down off that mountain and tore his tent to shreds. The missionary packed his bags and left in a hurry."

Reinhard had confidently replied, "That will never happen to us." But now, as he stood in the battered tent with mud rushing in underfoot and the steel masts lurching drunkenly as giant gusts of wind struck the canvas, those bold words of his seemed pretty empty. From the start, the weather had been against them. The tentmaster worked day and night to maintain it. Sleeping was almost impossible as the wind buffeted the trailers like a row boat on an open sea. Early one morning, one of the masts had collapsed and a huge valley formed in the tent roof with twenty tons of water in it that threatened to bring everything down with it.

He admits that his spirit was submerged in despair when he looked around him. All those years of praying and believing God for the tent, all the months of negotiations and work, and all the money — those were the thoughts that raced through his mind. The tentmaster said there was only one solution: to slash the canvas and let the water pour through. So that is what they did.

Reinhard had said, however, "We are not going to take down the tent. In the name of Jesus, we will continue." They continued, but so did the rain. Roads became impassable, bridges were washing away, still a few dozen people came to the services each night. Up until the night when the entire tent threatened to come down, they had been "limping to victory." Now it looked as if defeat was about to overcome them. As he watched the crew working to avert a disaster, a man came up to him. A resident of the Sibasa area, he had been saved and healed of a stomach ailment in the previous year's crusade.

He looked up at Reinhard with a brightness in his eyes and said, "Pastor, didn't you preach that all things are possible to them that believe?"

The challenge and boldness of the words struck Reinhard as a rebuke. Where was his much-vaunted faith? Yes, that was what he preached and what he believed! He replied, "Yes, you are right. I did not only preach it, I believe it in my heart." As he said those words, something began to happen. It was like waking up from a bad dream and realizing that all is well. The cobwebs of doubt were blown away as a breath of Holy Spirit power surged into his spirit. He looked around at the apparently pathetic and helpless situation, and repeated the words of Jesus, **All things are possible to him that believes** (Mark 9:23).

The cloud of gloom lifted, and he called the crew together to tell them, "I relieve you of all responsibility if anything goes wrong. In the name of Jesus, I accept full responsibility. This tent is not going to be taken down. We are going to stay here and continue to preach the Gospel."

Although there was incredulity on every face, faith grew in the hearts of the team members. Suddenly, they knew things would be all right, even if their eyes and their minds told them that disaster was less than a rain-drop away. They began to carry on with the mammoth task of keeping the tent up or, rather, keeping it afloat! Within a very short time, a miracle happened. The rain stopped, and the wind subsided. The hush of silence brought a quiet peace to everyone's heart and a holy awe.

A resounding victory crusade followed as they praised the Lord for intervening. The sun came out at last from behind a blanket of dingy, grey clouds. The muddy ground dried out, and like an army of ants on the move, the people appeared from over the hills. Down the stony paths and through the open veld, they snaked their way to the tent. As the meetings went on, there were more people outside than inside. It was an amazing, fantastic triumph for the Gospel as the Holy Spirit moved mightily on the people.

Reinhard renewed his acquaintance with the President of Vendaland when he and several other dignitaries attended one of the closing meetings. The President watched in amazement when some fifteen hundred people were bowled over by the power of the Holy Spirit and began to speak in other tongues. He leaped to his feet and asked, "Pastor, what power is this?" Reinhard grinned and replied, "Your Excellency, what you see is the power of the Holy Spirit." Later, the President took him aside and asked him to consider returning for a future crusade.

When the trucks creaked and bumped along carrying the tent to its next site, the Njelele mountain was bathed in sunshine. The local people no longer lived in fear. They had a new song: "Jesus is stronger than the mountain demons." As they were leaving, some village women came running out of the bush and knelt in front of the vehicle, begging him not to leave until they had heard the Gospel.

Faith won a mighty victory at Njelele, but it was not the last spiritual warfare the ministry had with satanic forces.

At the next big crusade held in Potgietersrus in April, a young man sauntered down the aisle between the long line of wooden benches paying little attention to the singing. When he saw the white preacher, however, hatred and anger welled up inside him.

The man admitted afterward that he had no intention of listening to the sermon. "Man, when I saw that white skin, all I could think of was murder. I came into the tent to have a look at the girls and to pick out one for myself, but as I looked around a voice suddenly spoke just behind me. I heard the words, 'Jesus loves you.'

"I whirled around, but I couldn't see who had said those words to me. But a sudden change came over me. I felt as though I was in the presence of God. I thought to myself, 'There is not a single person on this earth who loves me. Who would love me? Jesus?'

"I was rooted to the spot. I listened to the white preacher, and when he called people forward to give their hearts to Jesus, I ran out with tears pouring down my face. Jesus loved me and died for me."

The young man came onto the platform and threw his arms around Reinhard, hugging him as hot tears stained his cheeks. It was a wonderful transformation. Like Saul of Tarsus, he had been breathing threats of murder against the saints. Now he bowed in surrender to the Lord Jesus Christ. The change in his life was instantaneous. He had seven girl friends and went to each one, telling them his affair was over.

The next time Reinhard heard from this young man, he was at Bible school preparing to spread the good news about the love of God. Today, he is a minister of the Gospel.

Faith and Fear Fight a Deadly Duel

In July of 1978, after a couple of other crusades, a tour of Germany, and the dedication of the headquarters at Witfield, Reinhard held an evangelistic seminar at a place called Greenvalley in the northeastern Transvaal. Greenvalley became an arena in which faith and fear fought out a deadly duel, and there was only one winner.

The trucks and tent crew had gone ahead to set up, but almost immediately called back to the office to report poor ground conditions. Everything would be fine, if it did not rain. If it rained, however, there would be a catastrophe — the whole tent would collapse. The tentmaster was remembering the harrowing experiences at Njelele. Reinhard calmly spoke into the phone, "Pitch the tent. In the name of Jesus, it is not going to rain. It is not going to storm." He did not realize it, but he had just thrown down the gauntlet. His boldness would not escape without being tested.

When he arrived at the tent, he saw a pastoral scene with some lean-looking goats and sheep. Then as the sun went down behind the green hills, people came streaming down the little winding paths. The night air was filled with the chatter of thousands of men, women, and children making their way to the tent. Attendance was about eight thousand each night, and by the end of the seventeen-day crusade, more than eight thousand had filled in decision cards. In the meantime, a spiritual struggle occurred that was brief but stupendous in its outcome, not just for Greenvalley but probably for Africa.

On the eighth day, Reinhard was huddled over his Bible in the privacy of his trailer when a blast of wind buffeted it. The daylight began to get as hazy as if a filter were being pulled over the sun. As he stepped outside and looked toward the mountain range in the west, he gasped. Black clouds were rolling up, and a fierce wind was pulling them across the sky like huge sinister coils. There was no doubt that the devil had challenged his faith, and catastrophe was stampeding towards him in the form of a giant thunderstorm.

As he stood on the grass with the first gusts of cool, moist wind ruffling his hair, the Holy Spirit spoke to him and said, "Speak to the devil. Rebuke the devil." Reinhard tells what happened next:

"So I began to stride toward those angry looking clouds. I raised my finger, and I shouted, 'Satan, in the name of Jesus, I want to talk to you. Devil, if you destroy this tent of mine, I am going to trust God for another one three times the size of this one!' My words drifted across the open veld, and then something almost unbelievable happened before my very eyes. The wind and the rain parted to the left and to the right, making a wide detour around our tent. The storm never touched us. As I stood there, the Holy Spirit whispered again, 'See? Faith frightens Satan.'

"I was excited. I had met the enemy's challenge head-on, and he had been defeated by the authority of Jesus. Yes, the devil had been frightened out of his socks. Faith frightens Satan. What a wonderful truth! No wonder the Word of God says that our faith is more precious than gold, and the shield of faith quenches the fiery darts of the enemy. Faith puts Satan and his hellish hordes to flight. Praise God!

"As I stood there, however, a perplexing thought came into my mind about this strange thing that had happened which was really spiritual warfare in heavenly places. Perhaps I had not made myself clear to the devil. Maybe there was a misunderstanding. So I raised my voice again, and boldly said, 'Devil, in the name of Jesus, I want to talk to you once more. Although you withdrew the wind, and you withdrew the rain, that does not mean that I have made an agreement with you. I will still build a bigger tent anyway!'

"I needed to make it clear that I did not 'negotiate' any deals with the enemy. For God told us to cast him out, and that is what I intend to do as long as I live on this earth."

The seeds of faith for a super-large Gospel tent were sown in the fiery heat of spiritual battle at Greenvalley that September of 1978. Seeds were sown for no ordinary tent, but for the biggest tent ever seen on the face of the earth. It would be five more years before the mighty structure stood on the soil of Africa, but when it did, Christians everywhere gaped in wonder.

Satan on Crutches

During the last crusade of 1978 on the northern border of Lesotho and just afterwards, the evangelist received comfort and reassurance from one supernatural vision and a warning from another. God had been manifesting His power mightily with multiple healings and thousands saved when Reinhard suddenly saw Satan limping around the tent on crutches. The Holy Spirit said, "See — the enemy bears the sign of defeat." For Reinhard, that was a confirmation for his burgeoning ministry which now had thirty-two full-time members.

Toward the end of the year, he saw himself at the helm of a giant battleship. A splendid ship, it was heavily armored and massive guns looked out over the prow. As he looked ahead and down to the waterline, however, he noticed the ship was moving along a tiny river, hardly more than a brook, and up ahead was a sharp curve. He turned the wheel madly, but there was not enough water, and the ship became stuck fast in the mud.

When the vision ended, he puzzled over the interpretation. "Lord, what does this mean?"

In a flash, the answer came, "That is CFAN."

He caught his breath, and his heart began to beat faster. "Lord," he asked, "are we going to get stuck?"

Then came the interpretation. "A ship is carried by water. In the same way, Christ for All Nations needs to be carried by holy hands. Your base is too small. You need more holy hands to be lifted up on behalf of this work. Every single prayer partner constitutes one inch of this river. A battleship not only needs firepower, it needs maneuverability if it is to have success in battle."

That was a timely warning as the next few years would see the ministry locked in a deadly spiritual battle as the plan for the giant tent began to unfold. Prayer would be the key to the continued success and growth of the ministry. Reinhard took immediate steps after that vision to gain more prayer support, and since then, he has continually sought more and more people to back him prayerfully.

That crusade was in the beautiful mountain country of Qwa-Qwa. By now CFAN had invested in a sixty-four-seat bus, and its main use was to go to schools in the vicinity of crusades and bring the children to the meetings. During that crusade, one school principal refused to allow his pupils to be bused to the meetings. He believed CFAN represented some sinister religious sect.

One little girl slipped away from the school and attended anyway. She was slightly crippled in one foot and had to wear special shoes. When she reached the tent, she went quietly to a vacant spot on one of the benches to hear Pastor Kolisang. While she listened, a miracle happened. Her foot straightened out. She came back the next night and gave her testimony and also showed her principal what had happened. Shortly afterwards, he was in contact with CFAN:

"Bring your bus. Please take the children to the meetings," he enthused. That incident proved to be a breakthrough, because during the next few days, hundreds of schoolchildren made decisions for the Lord. In fact, entire busloads of children returned to their boarding schools saved. No wonder Reinhard had seen Satan limping around on crutches!

A Spiritual Desert Where Witchcraft Ruled

During 1979, spiritual warfare continued with especially heavy attacks by satanists and efforts by demons to disrupt the services.

In July and August, the caravan of trucks and vehicles rolled into Gazankulu. The equipment could hardly be seen for the clouds of powdery dust that hung in the air. It had not rained in many months, but what they found among the people was even worse: The place was a spiritual desert where fear and witch-craft ruled.

Night after night, the services were interrupted when people suddenly let out the most chilling shrieks.

Even during the day, people would be wandering around the big tent moaning and groaning. At night, Reinhard and the team got very little sleep because of the sinister atmosphere and the ear-piercing screams that occasionally rent the air. It was like being awake in the middle of an awful nightmare.

Reinhard recognized that a tremendous battle was going on in the supernatural as the Holy Spirit moved to set people free. The demonic forces were being provoked and manifested themselves with awful cries. He was curious, however, why so much demon power was being concentrated around the tent. One day, he visited a nearby village, a series of lopsided mud huts with grass roofs. In addition to the regular dwelling places, there were dwarf-size huts. Examining one of these, he found it filled with witchcraft fetishes and strange writings. The tiny huts were, in fact, shrines built especially for demon spirits. It seemed that most of the villagers had bound themselves to the demons. Now that they were hearing the Gospel, they wanted to be free, but the demons were reluctant to leave the victims they tormented and held captive.

The case of one young girl is typical of what happened during this crusade. She came eagerly to hear the Gospel, but as soon as she entered the tent, she went into a frenzy. They prayed for her, but it seemed she could not get released from the evil powers that possessed her. Pastor Kolisang went to her hut and found, as he suspected, a large cache of fetishes and other witchcraft items. The moment those things were removed and burned, the girl became completely free.

That experience caused Reinhard to urge all new Christians to renounce the past and surrender any idols, magic potions, or occultic items that may have been a part of their previous lives. He has seen over the years that, unless those things are totally destroyed, their owners never seem able to get free of demonic influence. Even yet, the platform in his giant tent is littered with all kinds of objects after an altar call. Many strange objects are hauled out and destroyed. This step of renouncing the past should not be confined to Africa. Many occultic symbols and practices permeate the American culture, such as astrology, and many newborn Christians do not have any idea those objects of jewelry and art can maintain a satanic influence in their lives.

Reinhard also learned more about the deliverance ministry. In his early encounters with demonic forces, he used to run from one person to another, trying to pray and cast out the demons.

"I used to be jumping everywhere, and I would fall into bed exhausted at night," he says, "I realized that if I continued like that, I would not make it to forty years of age. I then learned to have faith in the Holy Spirit and to let Him move in."

During the years, he has often been challenged by satanic forces, at times without even being aware of it. Satanists admit that they have deliberately come into his tent meetings with the intention of causing chaos. He was told once that four satanists sat in four different sections and attempted to call up demons to oppose him while he was preaching. The demons, however, would not manifest themselves inside the tent.

"I was told one satanist said the demons raced around the outside of the tent. They could not enter because it was encircled by a wall of fire," he relates.

Another time, several satanists came into the meeting accompanied by a witch highly rated for her ability to cast spells. As she tried to cast a spell, she began to shake from head to foot and shouted to her companions, "Get me out, get me out." One of the satanists, seeing this, reasoned that Jesus is more powerful than Lucifer or any witch and decided to renounce the devil and become a child of God. He later told Reinhard of the plan to disrupt the service.

Demonic disturbances are not confined to Africa. Once in Germany, a young Swiss woman sitting near the front at a meeting, jumped to her feet suddenly and screamed. Reinhard recalls, "It sounded as if there were a thousand demons in her. She ran up the aisle and out the door. The meeting froze as though somebody had opened a giant freezer, then one lady stood up and said, 'Pastor Bonnke, I am dead scared.'

"Then the Lord spoke to me, 'I have allowed this to happen to demonstrate my power.' I looked at the audience and said, 'How many of you will rise up with me in living faith and command these demons to leave that girl right now? She is outside, but that does not matter because the Holy Spirit is able to minister to her.' The entire congregation rose, and in the name of Jesus, we rebuked the devil and gained the victory. A few minutes later, the door reopened and that girl came in completely free. She was baptized in the Holy Spirit the same day."

His years of experience in Africa have made him fearless when it comes to facing demonic attacks. "I am not afraid of the devil, I believe he is afraid of me," he says with a confidence that takes some people aback. He was put to the test in Birmingham, England, in 1981.

He received a strange letter with no name. The signature was 666 and some other strange lettering.

It read, "Bonnke, you have invaded our territory. If you don't leave within two days, we are going to bring a curse down on your life."

His reaction was typical, "You won't succeed in chasing me out. I will chase you out of Birmingham."

A few days later, another letter arrived signed 666 which he did not even read but tore up and threw away remarking, "Devil, I don't read your epistles. I read God's epistles. I am not on the run. The gates of Hell are being blasted." He never received any further notes.

He did receive a nasty shock during a crusade in 1979. As repentant sinners streamed forward during the altar call, he urged them to throw witchcraft objects, liquor, and tobacco up onto the platform. As he dodged the items being thrown, what looked like a thick cable came sailing toward him. The "cable" landed close to his feet and began to wiggle. It was three poisonous snakes. Song leader Mtsweni grabbed the microphone stand and, with the help of others, clubbed the snakes to death. The man who threw them had inherited the snakes from his parents and used them for witchcraft practices. Now he wanted to follow Jesus and have nothing to do with those things anymore.

Can Jesus Heal a Broken Heart?

That year was marked by many more miracles and healings, which were different kinds of battles with satanic forces. One particular instance was the man with the broken heart. He was driving along the road on a motorbike when he saw the trucks with the sentence written along the side: "Jesus heals broken hearts." The young man stopped at the camp and hunted up the evangelist.

He said, "I didn't want to turn in here, but I did. I have a broken heart. Do you think Jesus could heal my broken heart?" Then he told his story:

"Seven years ago, I gave my life to God. I found Jesus as my Savior. I was delivered from all my evil habits and addictions. Then one day my wife went off for a few days to visit her parents. I was at loose ends and went for a walk. As I wandered along the street, I found myself in front of a place I had visited many times before I met Jesus.

"I was drawn like a magnet to that place. I couldn't resist it. I stood there wanting to go inside, but I couldn't because I felt the presence of Jesus with me. As I stood there, I folded my arms and said, 'Dear Lord Jesus, please leave me for five minutes so I can go in and do what I want to do.' When I came out of that house, Jesus was gone, and I have been alone with my misery and heartbreak for seven long years.

"Things have gone from bad to worse — seven times worse. I am down and out, crushed and broken. Do you think Jesus could ever help me again?"

As Reinhard listened to the man and looked into his pleading eyes, his own heart went out to him. He had to do something. Silently he prayed, and then the revelation came.

Looking at the young man, he said, "Listen, I will tell you what to do, and I will help you do it. I want you to take my hand and walk with me in the spirit back those seven years, back through the streets of that town and to that place where you prayed that fatal prayer for Jesus to leave you. I want you to kneel down and say, 'Lord Jesus, I revoke that prayer. Forgive me. I revoke that prayer.' "

The two then knelt down, and the man began to shout out his prayer. "Lord Jesus, I withdraw, I revoke that prayer. Forgive me." He wept, but now the tears were not the dregs of bitterness but showers of joy. Half an hour later, he leaped onto his motorbike, still weeping, but with heaven in his heart.

Every crusade has its highlights, and each has its own characteristics. For this reason, it is hard to judge one as more successful than another. But the November campaign of 1979 must rank as one of the best that year. It lasted nineteen days and produced twelve thousand decisions for the Lord. Not one single crime was reported to the local police during the crusade, and there were many healings and miracles. Among the thousands who accepted Jesus were Paramount Chief Justus Sigcau and his sister Stella, both members of the Transkei Parliament.

7
THE DAY OF THE COMBINE

This is no longer the day of the sickle, this is the day of the combine.

Early in 1979, after the Lord spoke those words to Reinhard, he decided to go ahead with plans to build a tent three times the size of his yellow one. His experience since he had moved from the traditional missionary stance to that of a mass evangelist had proven there was a great harvest of souls to be reaped for the Lord. He had made brief visits to Nigeria and to Kenya, and had seen the same hunger for the Word of God. He believed God wanted him to obtain a thirty-thousand-seat tent to be carried all over Africa for crusades.

The vision for Africa that had begun as a gentle breeze now was a hurricane in his heart. He confesses, however, that as the size of the tent project became embedded in his spirit, he had to switch off his mind — it was just too much to grasp. But he received great encouragement from reading in the Book of Romans that Abraham **staggered not at the promise of God** (Rom. 4:20).

The thought struck him, "It is not that we *cannot* stagger, but that we *must not* stagger in staggering situations." He determined then to go ahead with the project, and not to doubt but to trust God to provide the money.

An engineer and dedicated Christian, J.J. Swanepoel got down to the task of designing the tent, with no existing structure on which to model it. The size envisaged was far greater than any mobile tent man had ever designed, although a similar-sized stationary tent had been erected in Saudi Arabia.

The scale model made from the first drawings looked more like a spider's web with cables and ropes suspended from giant poles than it did a tent. The roof level was low, however, and except for the forest of hanging cables, the design was much like a conventional tent. The cost, however, would run more than a million dollars for construction, transportation, electricity, and other accessories needed. The fabric, of course, would have to be manufactured overseas. Negotiations began with companies in Hong Kong and in Milan, Italy.

Because of the novelty of such a tent, the Italian firm was prepared to cut its profits to get the job, so the engineer made several trips to Italy for talks. The Italians thought it would be possible to erect the suspension tent on the road in six to eight hours, using a crew of thirty men and up to a thousand pegs to anchor it. But, after some necessary design changes, even Brother Swanepoel admitted, "It is obvious that we underestimated the size of the engineering feat."

While the tent was being designed, a string of rallies and crusades were held with many souls saved followed by many supernatural healings, such as a hunchback being straightened as a young girl was healed of Sherman's disease. The focal point of that period, however, was the five-month campaign in Zimbabwe in 1980.

During Reinhard's last visit to that country in 1975, there was still a lot of fighting going on. He had seen the ravages of war and the persecution many Christians were suffering. After that, he had been under pressure to hold a crusade, but had refused because he felt the time was not right. In 1980, however, he had a witness from the Lord that the time was right.

Clearance for all the trucks and equipment had to be arranged at the border post, but then the CFAN convoy rolled across the wide Limpopo River. Forty local pastors from various denominations joined together to support the crusade and supplied a thousand workers to help with counseling and follow-up work.

After years of armed struggle, there was a real sense of spiritual hunger in the land, and the team expected great things. They were not disappointed. After only three nights in the first location, the yellow tent was overflowing. The altar call the first night was the largest they had ever seen. At this point, they had to move the crusade to the thirty-thousand-seat sports stadium nearby. It was mid-winter and chilly at night, but that did not seem to stop the people. The tent was left up and used as temporary living quarters by people coming from distant areas. They cooked their meals on small fires outside the tent and turned the benches into sleeping platforms at night.

On the last night of that first meeting, some five thousand people came forward to receive the baptism of the Holy Spirit. The night air was filled with the voices of thousands praising God in heavenly tongues. Many lay on the ground oblivious. It was a Day of Pentecost for Harare, Zimbabwe.

At the second location, a school principal gave this eye-witness account:

"When the advertisements first came out, people were not overly impressed. We had heard about so-called 'miracle workers' before, but nothing had happened. After Pastor Bonnke preached, however, it was clear that he was endued with power. The demonstration of the power of God through healings and salvation stunned the multitudes.

"I saw drunks giving their lives to God, drug addicts throwing away drugs and cigarettes, and witch-doctors renouncing their profession and throwing the 'magic medicines' onto the platform — an experience never seen here before."

As the five-month crusade went on in various locations, work continued slowly on the tent. Tests were carried out on the circular model, which proved unsatisfactory in high wind. Back on the drawing boards, the round tent now became an oblong tent. A thirteenth mast was added, but this caused problems and later was eliminated. An American engineering firm, Geiger and Burger Associates, was now involved with Brother Swanepoel. Also, of course, costs had started to climb, partly because of inflation and partly because the usual plastic fabric had been replaced with a glassfiber cloth coated with silicone rubber. The new fabric would not stretch and was admirably suited to the tension structure design. The original estimate of ten or twelve trucks also had been revised upward to nineteen, which alone cost more than a million dollars.

Reinhard had thought at first that eighteen months would see the tent completed, but in the end, it took more than three years. It was 1984 before the tent was dedicated. A pioneer project, this was like building a cavernous sports stadium, then folding it all up neatly, putting it away in containers, unpacking it at another place, and putting it all together again. The engineers admitted later there were times when they doubted if it could ever be done. In the meantime, the crusades continued.

The Soweto Witchdoctor

Reinhard had received many calls urging him to hold a campaign in the Soweto area. Since the bicycle brigade mission in 1975, he had gotten a negative answer from the Lord when he prayed about going to the "poor man" at the gates of Johannesburg. In March 1981, however, he was given a green light from the Holy Spirit. The welcome and response were overwhelming, and after a three-week break, the crusade continued in April and May. The first few nights, the crowds were small.

The breakthrough was the salvation of the woman who had been Soweto's chief witchdoctor for ten years. Actually, her influence had spread beyond the borders of South Africa. The congregation stared in disbelief as she shuffled down the aisle and called for a knife to cut off the strings of beads entwined around her colorful dress, the goatskin bracelets, and the fetishes that were the earmarks of her office. The news of her conversion spread like wildfire among the thousands of workers who travel into the city by train each morning. Although Soweto residents are highly sophisticated when compared to those in rural districts, the witchdoctor still wields as much power in the city as in the country.

The next night, the tent was filled to capacity, and the second night after her conversion, the crowd overflowed. So they moved the meeting next door into the sports stadium. The dark, unlit streets were alive with people praising the Lord, and the muggers and thieves seemed to melt away. White people, who normally were afraid to venture into Soweto after dark, also turned out for the meetings. Local church leaders were astonished and thrilled. Deliverance from demonic forces occurred at every service as the wind of the Spirit refreshed and revived the place.

The witchdoctor had not been a servant of Satan all of her life. She explained that shortly after her husband died, "he" had appeared to her in visions and instructed her to become a witchdoctor. For some time, she resisted but became seriously ill. Visits to doctors and hospitals were in vain. She then did the only thing she thought possible to regain her health — submit to the evil spirits. The day after making this decision, she had a visit from another witchdoctor who lived in Durban, hundreds of miles away. He claimed to have been sent by ancestral spirits to prepare and train her for her office. Apparently very "gifted" supernaturally, her powers were quite astonishing, and people began to come from all parts of the country to visit her for cures.

Unknown to the woman, however, one of her daughters had been saved in 1977 and had been fasting and praying for her mother's salvation. When the Bonnke crusade began, she invited her mother to the meeting.

"I didn't want to come," the former witchdoctor told Christian workers later, "I did not believe in the things my daughter did."

· But the daughter was persistent and kept begging her to attend "just one meeting." When she saw her mother go forward, she cried for joy and thanked God. "I had wept many tears before the Lord for my mother. God was faithful. Now I have a new mother," she said.

To prove that her past was wiped out and her sins forgiven, the erstwhile witchdoctor burned all her dry bones, medicines, herbs, and other black magic charms in a huge bonfire which was publicized by a local Sunday newspaper. The front page photograph of the fetishes going up in flames was a remarkable testimony of God's grace and of His power to overcome the forces of darkness and to bring light and life into a life ruled by fear and evil spirits.

Reports of healings and conversions were many, as was usual in the crusades, and one Saturday night, more than three thousand people came forward to receive the baptism in the Holy Spirit. It looked as if a giant wave had swept through the stadium as people were knocked off their feet. Miracles, spiritual and physical, were the only topic of discussion, and once and for all, Soweto knew that Jesus is alive. Even one minister discovered he was not saved and gave his heart to the Lord!

On May 10, 1981, the final service of a truly sensational crusade ended. The tent came down, the masts were loaded up, and the trucks rumbled along the streets and back to the Witfield headquarters. Reinhard would be returning to Soweto, however, for a third crusade, and this time he would set up the world's largest tent.

"I Will Give You a Sign"

The site where the factory to build the tent had been constructed proved too small, and a neighboring plot of ground had to be purchased. The first shipment of the new cloth covering had arrived, and the steel work was going ahead on schedule. Funds had to be there to pay for each phase of work.

Reinhard wrote his prayer partners: "The Lord has graciously supplied our needs so that we are able to continue construction on the new tent as fast as possible. My policy is, and remains, that we are not taking loans from banks or private individuals, but trust God, to whom silver and gold belongs."

The financing of the phenomenal tent was a miracle from its earliest beginning. In Germany once, Reinhard had taken with him a brochure and a model of the tent to display in the foyer of the auditorium. He shared his vision with the people, but made it very clear he was not there to beg for money.

"I don't ask for money," he told them, "I pray for it."

Throughout his ministry he has emphasized that people giving money to the project were not giving it to him, but to God.

During a prophetic utterance in that meeting, the Lord said, "I will give a sign today."

Reinhard knew the message mainly had to do with signs of healing and deliverance and was for the congregation, but he hastily whispered, "Lord, you know I need a sign as well." The financial pressures of the project plus the expansion of the ministry were beginning to be heavy.

After the service, a woman came up to him who had been saved the year before in one of his services. She said, "God has told me to give you some money for your new tent. I was sick at home and could not get to this conference, but last night I had a dream. I saw you stand and wave. I jumped out of bed, got into my car, and here I am. Here is a check for $12,500."

With that, she disappeared, while Reinhard stood open-mouthed, gaping at the check in his hand. Up to that time, it was the largest single donation he had ever received. He had received his sign from the Lord.

He made three other overseas visits in 1981, to Birmingham, England; to David Mainse's *100 Huntley Street* television program in Toronto, Canada; and to visit his sister in Calcutta, India. In Toronto, Mainse gave Reinhard an opportunity to make an appeal on the air. Instead of a financial appeal, the German evangelist made a spiritual appeal, "Pray for me. Pray for our ministry, and pray for the lost souls of Africa." Mainse, however, later raised $30,000 for the tent project.

Reinhard's only sister, Felicia, had qualified as a nurse and married an Indian doctor, Ronald Shaw. Both had joined Mark Buntain's famous mission in Calcutta. Before he arrived, Reinhard had been warned that the city of starving and dying millions also was the graveyard of great evangelists.

He said, "Well, I don't have to worry. I'm not a great evangelist."

Invited to preach in one of the city's largest Pentecostal churches, he was warned again not to expect miracles or anything great. His hosts said, "It must be the oppression which hangs over the city." Reinhard went to his room to pray, "Lord, they say they don't see miracles here. That is why I want to see miracles here in the name of Jesus."

When he walked into the church, he caught the scent of battle, not the scent of evil. It was something like a duel, so he didn't waste any time parrying with his opponent. He went straight onto the offensive and preached on faith. Soon there were "hallelujah's" ringing through the church. At the close, he called for the sick to come forward, specifically the blind. An elderly woman was ushered up to the front "as blind as a stone." He learned later that she was a "regular customer" for all visiting preachers.

With every eye in the church on him, he laid his hands on her eyes and prayed, "In the name of Jesus Christ, the Son of God, blind eyes open."

He stepped back, and she screamed, "I see, I see."

The pastors began to rejoice, and there was a move of the Holy Spirit that reminded him of the waves of power he had become accustomed to in southern Africa.

On the flight home, he met a young Buddhist businessman from Taiwan and they spent several hours talking about Jesus. By the time they parted at Jan Smuts Airport, the man was asking about how to receive Jesus, so Reinhard invited him over for dinner. Afterwards, the two knelt down and the man accepted Jesus as his personal Savior.

Also in 1981, there was a crusade in Zambia which meant rolling the convoy of trucks almost twelve hundred miles across Zimbabwe, the Zambesi River, and Zambia to Livingstone near the magnificent Victoria Falls. The crusade resulted in more than eleven thousand decisions for Christ, also an opportunity to talk with and pray for President Kaunda at the Zambia State House. A weary team returned to Witfield in December for a well-earned rest.

Progress was being made on the tent — not as fast as Reinhard would have liked — but at least there was progress. One of the seven-story masts had been raised, and he daringly climbed to the top of it. The rest of the masts and most of the steelwork had been fabricated, leaving only the welding to be done. More material had arrived from the United States, and the arduous task of glueing the computer-patterned panels together was beginning. A pressing need was a little over three miles of steel cable, which alone would cost about $45,000. The rest of the fabric also was expected in 1982. By the grace of God, the accounts were being met as Christians all over the world contributed to the project.

Because of its unique character, the project was being carried out by a small crew, which meant it was taking much longer than expected. The normal crusade expenditure, the upkeep and transport of the existing yellow tent, had to be sustained as well. In addition to finances, the evangelist's workload has increased each year. His first visit of 1982 was to Zaire where he met with church leaders and a man known to most Pentecostal Christians simply as Brother Alexander.

Having been colonized by Belgians, Zaire has a strong Roman Catholic background, but today a vibrant evangelical witness is sweeping through the country. In one area alone there were eighty-two Pentecostal churches, with more than twenty-five hundred churches having been founded in the seven years just previous to his visit. The Holy Ghost revival there, in fact, has many similarities to the Indonesian revival described by Mel Tari in his book, *Like a Mighty Wind*.

The people apparently had no difficulty in believing and expecting for even the most impossible miracles. That was how the great awakening began. Brother Alexander, a man with a very elementary education, began to pray for the sick who were healed.

Then one day, some people brought the body of a young woman into the service. Her fiance defiantly threw out a challenge, "You say God raises people from the dead. Here is a test for you."

She had been dead for four days, and Brother Alexander says the smell was almost unbearable. But he called the little congregation together around the corpse, and they began to praise and rejoice for about twenty minutes. Then he felt someone tug at his jacket and opened his eyes. He saw that the corpse was missing, and he looked around and spotted the "dead" woman standing among those praying with her eyes closed and hands raised, praising God. When the people saw her, they all ran out the door with Brother Alexander in hot pursuit! The miracle shook the area, and people turned to God in large numbers.

A Visit to South Korea

Early in 1982, Paul Yonggi Cho, pastor of the world-famous Central Full Gospel Church in Seoul, South Korea, invited Reinhard to visit. The evangelist was excited over the invitation and says he had a thousand questions for the man with the world's biggest church.

"I could hardly believe my own eyes. Dr. Cho told me the church grows at the rate of nine thousand people a month. The Sunday services were like an anthill. Beginning at 6 a.m., thousands of people flock in to hear the Word of God, then leave to be replaced by another group of thousands. I was told the church is growing four times faster than the natural population increase. If the momentum continues, by 1990 half of the population will be Christian," Reinhard told his staff when he returned.

The visit was a tonic for Reinhard, giving him visible reassurance that his goal — "Africa shall be saved" — really was possible. "When I saw what Dr. Cho was doing and how the Lord was blessing him, I said, 'Lord, I've trusted you for peanuts.' "

He returned to South Africa with his faith level high — which was just as well. Although the Big Tent was nearing its final stages, a giant cash problem was on the way. More material was needed for the completion of the panels, but the order could not be shipped until payment was made. If the final payment of $37,500 was not paid, the suppliers might cancel the entire contract. In that case, they would lose the $87,500 already paid.

A little money came in and they waited for the mail each day, expecting it to surely come that way. The deadline drew nearer, and it was an anxious time. Reinhard drew strength, however, from the fact that the project was not his.

"I never sat down and figured it all out. This is God's tent," he said, so he waited for "deliverance" to come.

Just two days before the deadline expired, the Bonnke family was just sitting down at the breakfast table when the phone rang. It was a long-distance call from a German man he had never met. The man's agitated voice said, "Pastor Bonnke, I cannot sleep at night . . . ."

At that point, the evangelist thought someone was calling for prayer, so he asked what the problem was.

But the man continued, "Pastor Bonnke, when I close my eyes at night, all I see in front of me is your face! I hear a voice saying, 'Pastor Bonnke needs money.' Is that true?"

Reinhard's spirit began to ring with hallelujahs as he said, "Yes, that is so."

The man asked urgently, "How much do you need."

As calmly as he could, Reinhard answered, "I cannot tell you. If I tell you the amount, you will think I am being cheeky."

Back came a despairing plea, "Please, Pastor Bonnke, tell me. I *must* know the amount."

"Well, all right. I need $37,500 right now," said Reinhard.

There was a silence, broken only by a crackle across the telephone wires, then came a stunning reply, "I will transfer it today."

The mysterious caller, a Roman Catholic, was as good as his word, and the money was duly transferred permitting him to get a good night's sleep! Breakfast at the Bonnke house was turned into a thanksgiving banquet as they rejoiced at the eleventh-hour deliverance.

When telling this story, Reinhard adds, "I slept like a baby, because I knew the Lord would not let us down. Yet the man who had the money could not sleep."

It was a spectacular and miraculous financial provision, but the need had stretched the faith of many of the team to the breaking point. Their "daily bread" is not always provided in such a startling way, of course. With thousands of faithful prayer partners scattered across many lands, money often comes in small amounts. In his meetings, Reinhard trusts the Holy Spirit to gently move the hearts of the unrepentant to repentance and to, just as gently, move on the hearts of people to give. He trusts God to supply all of his needs.

One pastor said, "When I hear Bonnke preach, my hand is itching to give. But when I hear some other men preach, I often feel like going up to them and asking for a little credit."

After the cash crisis, the hard-working tent crew took a deep breath and plowed on at the task. It had been three years since the plans were drawn, and even some of the staunchest prayer partners were beginning to doubt the wisdom of the tent. The tent itself was still within the budget, but the additional equipment and transport, with inflation, had skyrocketed the total need amount to $1.125 million. At the same time, the headquarters needed expanding. An adjoining property was purchased with a large house which was to be expanded to provide accommodation for the extra full-time staff needed with the new tent, as well as room for the transport fleet.

Several volumes could be filled with hundreds of fascinating and faith-building stories of changed lives, deliverance from evil, and physical healings that occurred during that period. Each incident was very precious to Reinhard, but when he looks back at that time, only one event is clearly etched into his mind — the Big Tent.

8

THE BIG TENT TAKES SHAPE

From the day in 1979, when the first sketch was made, Reinhard had been unflagging in his zeal and determination to see the tent project carried through to the end. At times, it looked like an impossible dream to even the men who worked on it, and as the tent neared completion, they began to breathe sighs of relief that their work had not been in vain.

Toward the end of 1982, a large piece of land was leased for a test site, and the crew began ferrying the steel masts, the miles of steel cable, the truck loads of shackles, bolts, and chains, the massive main anchors, and the precious roof material from the factory to the test site. The test erection was to involve only six of the masts. Test drilling had to be done to find the right place, because half the ground was of a soft, clay composition, and on the northern extreme of the site the drillers hit solid rock. Once the anchors had been secured and some hitches ironed out, the next big job was raising the masts.

Six giant cranes were moved onto the plot of land, which had begun to take on the appearance of a wharf-side quay. At the end of the appointed day, however, there was a collective cheer as six of the seven-story-tall masts stood pointing heavenward. Reinhard had been out of town and did not know the masts were up until he caught a glimpse of them as he drove home along the freeway. Something new and unfamiliar caught his eye, and he looked again. Then it dawned on him that he was looking at part of his Big Tent.

"My soul was flooded with happiness, and tears rolled down my cheeks as I thanked God from the bottom of my heart for this miracle," he says.

A lot of hard work and perspiration went into the job of pumping up the fabric with a hydraulic jack, but by nightfall, the tent covering was waving gently in the breeze with only the job of tightening the cables left for the next day. A tremendous rain storm with high winds and hail hit the area that night and tons of water were trapped in the fabric, but damage was slight. Technical problems developed with the section designed for the pulpit and platform area, however, and finally this section was dispensed with — which eliminated that thirteenth mast.

All the activity had caught the attention of local newspapers and, as far away as Durban, full page stories ran on the "Seventh-Story Heaven," as the headline read. More people were taking notice of the tent as a "world's first" of its kind, including a British technical journal. After four years, the tent — even if it was only a section of it — stood next to a main freeway as a symbol of God's supernatural provision of finances and a sign of the faith of a man who was prepared to dare anything for Jesus.

Engineers wanted to carry out more tests, especially those connected with safety before clearing the tent for its first campaign. From the brief experience gained in moving the masses of equipment from one site to another, and from the time it had taken to prepare the site and to dismantle the section, one thing became very obvious. Transportation, in quantity, was needed very badly. The technicians also wanted at least one more trial run before opening the Big Tent for a full crusade.

Meetings on Four Continents

Reinhard's schedule continued to expand. His crusade organizers could hardly cope with the invitations, nationally and internationally. The year began with a crusade at Pretoria, South Africa, then he went to Australia, where twenty-six Pentecostal churches cooperated in a meeting held at Auckland. The local paper ran a headline that said, *Fiery Evangelist 'Plunders Hell to Populate Heaven,'* and ran interviews with people who had been healed under the Bonnke ministry.

Also, news media representatives were beginning to ask questions about political attitudes in South Africa, but none of the CFAN team allowed themselves to be drawn into those discussions.

Reinhard's polite answer always was, "I am not part of the problem. I am part of the solution. I am an ambassador for Jesus and not for any country."

Back in South Africa, crusades began again in the smaller yellow tent and in sports stadiums. One of these meetings, at Dennilton, was marked by a considerable amount of demonic manifestation, a reminder once again that the battle is not against flesh and blood, but against spiritual forces.

In March, he made a month-long tour of America. While in Houston, Texas, he received a call that the yellow tent had been blown down. At the time, that was a serious problem because it was his only workable crusade structure. One consolation was that apparently no one had been hurt. He spent an anxious night in prayer, not knowing all the details of the accident. Later, he found that it had occurred after services in Northern Transvaal had ended, but while new Christians were being taught nightly as part of the regular follow-up procedures. A fierce wind suddenly came up and, although the crew immediately began to let down the side walls and tighten up the ropes, they could not contend with the wind. Apparently they were hit by a freak tornado, which is extremely rare in that area. Suzette Hattingh, head of CFAN's women's ministry was on the platform at the time and described what happened:

"The wind hit the tent, and it seemed to blow up like a balloon and then deflate. It inflated a second time, and then everything seemed to come loose. The main iron beam running across the centre of the tent lifted. Tent poles also lifted, and everything began to rattle and fall. It was like watching a tidal wave in slow motion, a tidal wave of yellow canvas, cables, lights, and poles.

"I have never seen so many people move so quickly to get out of a tent. I am sure the angels must have helped them out. A mast at the back of the tent twisted and collapsed, and the one above the platform where I was standing began to bend like a bow. I remember our organist doing a somersault over the edge of the platform and disappearing into the night. Moments later, I found myself almost alone in the tent, and in the background an automatic, melodic beat — it was the organ."

Richard Walters, an American member of CFAN who was in charge of follow-up work and now ministers in Nigeria, was trapped under the sea of canvas for a while but escaped unhurt. There was hardly any hysteria, despite the fact that many mothers and children had been separated in the wild exodus. Team members who visited the site the day after the storm were amazed at the destruction and even more amazed at the miraculous protection for the more than three thousand people who had been inside when the wind hit the tent.

At first, it appeared that the next crusade would have to be postponed, and it had already been advertised. Meanwhile, insurers were called in to assess the damage. It was estimated that the tent would be out of commission for at least two months while the shredded canvas was repaired. Reinhard decided to go ahead with the planned meeting and hold it in the open air. Being April, the weather was still warm at night. The only deterrent would be rain. The meeting was shortened to one week as a precaution. Night after night, long lines of people filed in to fill the benches under cloudless, starry skies. On the final night, almost twelve thousand people attended.

Reinhard next headed for Finland, stopping over in Denmark to preach in one of Copenhagen's largest Pentecostal churches and to connect with an Australian television crew who wanted to interview him, airing the message to thousands on that continent. When he arrived in Helsinki, it looked as if he were a candidate for general election. His name was plastered everywhere, and as he stood on the pavement outside his hotel, he even saw his name and photograph going past him on the side of a tram car. Huge billboard photographs peered down at him in the market square. The Finnish pastors had worked tirelessly preparing for the main crusade scheduled in an indoor ice stadium. He had never seen such wide publicity, including a "March for Jesus," through the main streets.

All the publicity naturally stirred up the print, radio, and television media, who turned out in force on opening night to see the visiting German evangelist from Africa and to find out why he was so popular. The press coverage turned out to be favorable, which was something of a surprise. The major afternoon daily newspaper carried the story on the crusade as its main front page story the next day with a headline of *Signs and Wonders Today*. At another location in Finland, a woman reporter asked him to pray for her and was slain in the Spirit — not an orthodox way to conduct an interview!

A popular secular magazine carried large pictures and a report on the meetings, and one reporter suggested in his column that members of the Finnish Parliament go to hear Reinhard Bonnke speak. The news of the crusade reached as far as Lapland, and Christian groups traveled hundreds of miles to attend some of the meetings.

The stadium in Helsinki was filled to its capacity of ten thousand people each night. There was one major difference in the crowds, however. Unlike the more emotionally uninhibited saints of the southern hemisphere, Scandinavians are much more reserved and cool in their religious fervor. By the time Reinhard left Finland, however, his enthusiastic preaching had thawed out the Finnish emotions, and "hallelujahs" were filling the halls wherever he spoke. When a gypsy woman on a pair of crutches gave them to Reinhard and began to jump and run one night, there was pandemonium as ten thousand people forgot their inhibitions.

Night after night, the crowds thronged forward to give their hearts to Jesus. Long lines of people waited for prayer. In fact, the lines became so long that he had the people arranged in two rows with a walkway between and moved down the rows laying hands on two people at a time. Once he looked in back of him to see everyone lying on the ground, and later quipped, "For a moment, it looked as if I had parted the Red Sea!"

When he left Finland, there was no doubt in Reinhard's heart, as he peered out of the airplane windows at the scenic beauty of the land of a thousand lakes, that the blessing of God had been poured out in a wonderful way. Now it was back to the land of his calling — Africa — where his next major crusade was a sharp contrast. The yellow tent, now repaired, was pitched in Botswana, which was in the grip of drought. From the crystal clear skies of Finland, it was a dramatic change to the African scene with clouds of red dust everywhere.

The Big Tent Is Tested

Crusades continued in South Africa during June and July. The Bonnke team returned to some places that had been visited in 1975 early in the crusade ministry. There were many happy reunions with people saved and healed in those earlier meetings. Several of them had established churches of their own.

Also, in June, he accepted an invitation to preach at Ray McCauley's Rhema Church in Randburg as part of a three-day seminar on healing. There was only one problem: he and several members of CFAN had arrived back home the day before from a crusade where they had picked up a severe virus. With family, friends, and colleagues interceding in prayer, Reinhard was able to make the seminar.

He went from Randburg to Durban for a three-day preaching blitz. Then he continued on to a rally at Chatsworth, where some four thousand people gathered on a soccer field to hear the Gospel of Jesus Christ preached in a predominantly Hindu-believing area.

When he boarded the plane to return to Witfield, he was a tired man. Although he knew he was pushing himself to the limit, he also knew that he had to keep on going. The vision had to be fulfilled.

Back at home for a few days, he was able to examine the progress on the Big Tent. The site chosen for the first trial was next to a large housing district where there were open grounds for parking. The plan was to raise nine of the twelve masts and activity was feverish.

August is not an ideal time to hold a crusade in that country because it is winter and the nights can be bitter, but the year's schedule made it imperative to run the crusade then. Otherwise, there would be no test possible before the official opening and Dedication Day, set for February 18, 1984.

A special service was held for the more than one hundred-member crew and office staff the day before the crusade opened. The voices of praise and worship were lost in the cavernous dome of the tent and they barely filled the first three rows of the center block. Reinhard told his staff, "The old CFAN is dead. We are moving into a new dimension."

As foreseen, the weather during the first two weeks in August was bitterly cold and obviously kept a lot of people indoors and away from the services. Despite this, attendance built from about three thousand the first night to an average of seven or eight thousand. The several hundred responding to the altar calls were "the first-fruits of a new harvest of souls for Africa," the evangelist said. About eight thousand people registered decisions for the Lord during the crusade.

The tent crew was satisfied with the trial run. They had been given the opportunity to test sound systems and lighting, and to check out the operation of a dozen other items. A lot of practical experience resulted and they were confident that Dedication Day in Soweto would not only be more streamlined in operation, but would see the tent filled.

Of course, the Big Tent was gobbling up the major portion of the ministry's finances. More transportation was needed, as well as drilling rigs, generators, video equipment, and many other pieces of equipment.

"God pays for the things he orders, and the Big Tent is not mine. It is His," was again Reinhard's prognosis. He is a man of faith, but also a man of works and prayer, and much prayer also was being sent up for the urgently needed trucks.

The American Connection Forged

Earlier in 1983, while the tent was still being completed, the kernel of an idea had begun to take root in Reinhard's mind, and a new word dominated his thinking for the rest of that year — strategy. Africa was the harvest field to which he was called, and despite the size and effectiveness of his ministry, he had started to realize that he needed more allies in this showdown with the devil for the salvation of a continent. He had a yearning to meet like-minded men and to share his vision with them, to gain their confidence and cooperation.

During his trip to the States, he had visited the famous evangelist, T.L. Osborn, in Tulsa, Oklahoma. Osborn, one of the all-time greats in mass evangelism, had campaigned in Africa with his wife, Daisy, particularly in Nigeria. Reinhard spent two hours with T.L. sharing mutual experiences, hopes, and plans for the future. Then he visited Freda Lindsay's Christ for the Nations Institute in Dallas, Texas, where he met with students, many of whom were from Africa. He was impressed with their desire to see Africa won for Jesus.

Out of the two meetings, a plan evolved. He was to host a conference of six hundred of Africa's top evangelists in Swaziland in October 1984. The meeting was to be called the "Fire Conference." With this conference idea burning in his heart, he went on to a conference in Holland, still busy meeting and contacting preachers from Africa.

At one meeting, he exclaimed, as he often does, "We will travel from Cape Town to Cairo with this Big Tent . . . ." Before he could finish, an Egyptian evangelist stood up with notebook and pen in hand to ask, "Tell me, Pastor Bonnke, when will you be in Cairo?"

The Amsterdam conference gave him his first opportunity to meet Dr. Billy Graham, who surprised Reinhard with his knowledge of CFAN's ministry. In fact, Dr. Graham told him he had recently received a personal report of the meetings in Finland which Bonnke had conducted not long before.

During those few weeks, valuable links had been forged with Christian television networks in America. Films of some of the African crusades had been flown over and the networks became excited about them. Christian Broadcasting Network (CBN), based in Virginia Beach, Virginia, contacted him about an interview which actually took place some months later. In the years to follow, he would appear on many American television programs and at special meetings and programs, such as Dr. Kenneth Hagin's annual Oklahoma campmeetings held in Tulsa's large convention center.

Despotism Cannot Destroy Christianity

Following the crusade trial run of part of the Big Tent, Bonnke went to Uganda for a three-day meeting. From the moment he arrived, he was struck with the depth of dedication of the Christians in Kampala, the Ugandan capital. While there, he stayed at the home of a high-ranking government official. His host had some fascinating and blood-curdling tales to tell about Idi Amin's reign of terror. Many of the accounts were first hand because his host had been an official in the Amin government.

During Amin's infamous reign more than a million people were murdered. Christians often had been in the frontline of his demonic hatred for human life. In the midst of all the carnage, Reinhard's host had survived, and at great personal risk saved countless Christians from being put to death. Amin had tolerated a section of the established church, but viciously opposed the Pentecostal/evangelical groups. House meetings were banned. The feared secret police periodically burst into houses and, if people were found in prayer or with Bibles, they were arrested. Amazingly, Reinhard's host had been put in charge of religious affairs. When he was told of an impending raid, he often would manage to get a message to the house groups to flee.

The three-day crusade had been widely publicized, but Reinhard and his co-workers were puzzled at seeing only a few of the hundreds of posters which had been sent on ahead. When they asked the organizers why posters were not on every street corner, they found that Christian literature was so scarce and the posters so attractive Christians were pulling them down and hanging them up in their homes as decorations.

From the very first meeting in the city square, just a stone's throw from the Supreme Court buildings, God's power was displayed. Healings were multiplied. The good central location backfired, however, and the next afternoon's meeting had to be canceled. Officials complained that noise had interrupted Court, and they had been forced to close their sessions.

The final meeting was on a Sunday afternoon, and about six thousand people showed up. Ominous black clouds began to gather and dust banks swirled toward the city while he was preaching. Not wanting to skip the altar call, Reinhard raced through his sermon and had hardly said "amen" when giant rain drops began to fall. He and some pastors took refuge in a parked vehicle, expecting the crowd to disperse. But the people just stood, soaked to the skin. Apparently they felt they could not be any wetter than they already were. The sight of the bedraggled crowd waiting patiently touched Reinhard's heart. He climbed back onto the platform in the rain and began to minister and pray for the sick.

In spite of all the persecution and hardship, Christianity is still very much alive in Uganda. The people were hungry for the Gospel. As a servant of God, he could not turn his back on those people. As his jet plane lifted off the ground, Reinhard looked out the windows searching for a site where he could bring the Big Tent and return for a full-scale crusade.

A Hunger for Spiritual Things

From Uganda, he was off to a month-long preaching tour in Germany after a few days at home in Witfield. Reinhard has faithfully returned to his Fatherland year after year. It has often been painful to his soul to see the spiritual famine in his country, and indeed, throughout western Europe. This time, however, he was pleasantly surprised to see a genuine hunger for the things of God and to see the numbers of young people responding to the offer of salvation.

"The young people are fed up with all the materialism that has surrounded them in the past. They want reality, and they are finding it in Jesus," he says.

While in Germany, the long-awaited interview on CBN took place. Because of his preaching schedule, it had to be conducted live via a satellite link-up from Germany. When he arrived at the studio in Stuttgart where his end of the interview was to originate, technicians were very curious to know why a preacher rated VIP treatment with a trans-Atlantic satellite interview. Such link-ups usually were only for politicans.

The interview, conducted by CBN's founder, Pat Robertson, went smoothly. The Holy Spirit clearly directed the theme. Viewers in America, waiting for the link-up with Reinhard in Germany, listened to

Robertson talking about the move of God across the world from the text of Joel 2:28: **I will pour out my spirit upon all flesh.** Reinhard had not heard any of the previous program, yet he opened his part of the interview with the same verse. This interview opened the way for a hectic television schedule throughout Canada and America in late 1983 when he and Robertson would meet face to face over a luncheon that would be of great significance to CFAN.

Back in Johannesburg, Reinhard gave the green light for Dedication Day for the Big Tent at a two-week crusade in Soweto, then took off with his general manager across the Atlantic on an energy-sapping four-week visit to Canada, America, and back to Germany.

As the year drew to a close, the urgency for the trucks to haul the Big Tent became greater. Cost, of course, was the main hurdle. Without transportation, however, the Big Tent was much like a huge whale stranded on the beach at low tide. Ever since a simple communion service at the trial meeting in July, Reinhard and the CFAN team had been praying and believing God for ten trucks by the end of December. Money for trucks had been promised by several churches, but the cash still had to come in. So the two men left in mid-November with a real urgency in their spirits for trucks.

The welcome and response Reinhard and Peter Vandenburg received across America was remarkable. They found that the vision and the mission of the Big Tent was a major item of discussion among American Christians. The television programs where they appeared were a great success. Reinhard was able to share personally with Pat Robertson much of his vision for Africa. Robertson pledged a substantial amount of money to CFAN for 1984, and another large amount was paid over immediately. Cash for the trucks was at last available.

The Lord had an even greater surprise and blessing waiting when the men arrived in Germany for a couple of quick meetings. Some time earlier, Reinhard had heard of a fleet of vehicles that had been ordered by the Libyan government but which had not all been accepted. Now he visited the vehicle depot in Hamburg and saw row upon row of new, six-wheel-drive trucks fitted with hydraulic winches. All of the equipment had been especially strengthened for North African conditions.

As he stared at the vehicles, he began to feel a surge in his spirit, and he was not wrong. The Holy Spirit had led him into one of the best financial deals of his life. The trucks were for sale — at half price. All he needed to do was respray them, as they were painted a somber military green. Not only was the price an outstanding bargain, but the United States dollar was riding high as well. The money contributed in America paid for six tractors and ten trailers.

He could not help smiling and praising God for this provision: "The swords of revolution are being beaten into plowshares for the Gospel. Maybe one day these self-same trucks will bring the Gospel to Libya."

9

THE WINDS OF WRATH

The main focus for early 1984 was the official dedication of the Big Tent. Inquiries began to flow in from around the world. Christians who had followed the saga of its construction over the years and contributed and prayed for the project wanted to be at the opening crusade. The site chosen was on the edge of sprawling Soweto with good access by road. Some initial obstacles had to be overcome, such as stringent rules by municipal authorities and some church leaders in Soweto who at first did not want to cooperate. Those hurdles were overcome by prayer and diplomacy and a spirit of unity was forged for the two-week crusade to follow.

The Big Tent continued to attract publicity at home and abroad. Even a *New York Times* reporter called to interview Reinhard. Obviously there was a need now for long-range planning and professional advertising, and an outside agency was called in to design a new logo and to advise on nationwide billboard advertising.

The preparation of the site for the pile-driving of the anchor system and the erection of twenty tons of fabric went off without any serious hitches. They had one scare, however, when a torrential storm with large hail stones peppered the area. Some of the roof panels had not yet been placed in the proper tension, and because of the complicated lifting system, it was not possible to lower them. The men watched anxiously as the wind, rain, and hail pounded the tent, but no serious damage was suffered. The crew became satisfied that the giant structure would be able to withstand future bad weather.

Several days before the February 18 dedication, Reinhard called a prayer meeting in the tent from 8 p.m. to midnight. All of the technical and administrative staff gathered among the sea of wooden benches and walked or knelt on the sawdust floor to intercede for the coming crusade. During the evening, a prophecy came through one of the team in which a warning to walk in humility and righteousness was given. Reinhard, obviously touched by the prophecy, emphasized again that this was not his tent nor his idea, that the tent was the Lord's and part of His divine purpose to save Africa. During the course of his informal address to the staff, he also talked about the necessity of giving one another proper love and recognition — and added that ministries were going to be born out of CFAN.

"Ministries will develop out of this Big Tent," he said and spoke about the five-fold ministries. Not even he realized how prophetic his own words were. Since then several men and women who were at that meeting have left to pioneer new churches and ministries for Jesus. It was an unusual way of addressing the staff for Reinhard, who usually was stressing that everyone on the team should submit to the unity of one vision and to operate in agreement. That, of course, was the vision of CFAN, the vision God had given Reinhard to win Africa for Jesus.

As a grand finale to the evening's prayer meeting, the staff joined for a "Jericho march" around the tent, ringing it with prayers for the salvation and deliverance of all who would ever step inside the mighty tent cathedral.

Dedication Day proved to be gloriously hot and summery, and from early morning thousands of vehicles and hundreds of buses began congregating at the site. A party of one hundred and thirty-nine Germans flew in for the special occasion, and arrangements were made for a translation booth to be set up. Others flew in from America, Finland, Britain, and Australia, while thousands more arrived from every part of southern Africa. One group traveled a thousand miles by bus from Cape Town to be at the service, arriving after lunch that day and leaving immediately after the service for the return trip of a thousand miles.

Officially, the Big Tent seated thirty-four thousand people, but it was full by lunchtime that day, and people still were arriving by the thousands. The program involved a praise festival during the morning with the official dedication service scheduled for 4 p.m. By that time, the aisles were clogged with people, and on one side, the tent flaps were lifted to allow several thousand more people to watch and hear the service. An estimated fifty thousand people attended, one of the biggest gatherings of Pentecostal Christians in the country.

The service was conducted by the Rev. Nicholas Bhengu, who in his early ministry had been called "Africa's greatest soulwinner" and who has now gone on to be with the Lord, and the Rev. Paul Schoch, a board member of Reinhard Bonnke Ministries in America. The main message was delivered by Reinhard, who has never relished too much pomp and ceremony. So his sermon, as usual, was a message on salvation and some five thousand people came forward at the altar call to accept Jesus. The service was a moving experience that few who were there will ever forget.

Reinhard said, "When the Lord first spoke to my heart about this mighty tent, the spiritual climate was not right, but we went ahead and started the project. It is always best to obey God. Today, the spiritual climate is right. Africa is hungry for the Word of God, and this Big Tent is ready to roll through Africa."

(His avowed intention to reach Cairo one day with the Gospel tent is as well-known to his partners as is his determination to achieve a goal. It would not be surprising to see another kind of "pyramid" nestling in the sands alongside the Nile River before the year 2000!)

One of several foreign journalists present at the dedication was Barry Chant, editor of Australia's New Day magazine. Afterwards he wrote in an editorial:

"I am certainly glad I was there. . . . I looked for the policemen that one would expect at such an event in volatile Soweto. I saw none." He also commented, "Bonnke read from Ezra 6:14 in the *Living Bible*, **The Temple was finally finished, as had been commanded by God** — the completion date for the temple had been February 18, the same date chosen for the tent dedication!"

The service did not end until after 7 p.m. What a day it had been. The event drew considerable international television coverage, as well as in newspapers and magazines. An American crew spent several weeks filming and producing a program that was later seen on several United States networks. Even a British BBC-TV news crew visited one night, and some of their footage showing some healings was aired on prime time newscasts in Britain and Australia, and in Zimbabwe and other African countries.

The two-week crusade produced a rich and bountiful harvest for the Lord in the form of some twenty-five thousand decisions registered. A large number of healings took place, although in comparison with other campaigns, the healings seemed disappointingly small. As in previous Soweto crusades, some witchdoctors were won to the Lord. One of them was a small, bright-eyed woman, Margaret Mphaga, whom it was hard to imagine drinking the warm blood of a freshly slaughtered goat in the initiation rites. But that is what she did, after she went to a witchdoctor for a cure for asthma and was pressed into becoming one herself "in order that no future illness or harm befall her."

She said, "I never liked the idea, but I was too afraid to say no."

She was brought to the tent by the prayers of her son and by his gentle persuasion. A Christian for twelve years and a Bible school graduate, he had been praying for his mother for the past nine years to be delivered from the evil influence of Satan. After she was saved on a Monday, her elderly mother was saved on Wednesday. At the Saturday evening service, she brought a huge pile of fetishes, stacked them on the platform, and made a public renouncement of her old lifestyle. Testimonies like hers hit home in the hearts of many thousands, and the people of Soweto began to stream nightly to the brightly lit tent to take hold of a new life.

Victory in Calcutta

On May 6, 1984, the people of Calcutta, India, were smothering under a blanket of hot, humid air with not even a whisper of wind to bring cool relief. The body heat of several thousand people crammed together in the grounds of St. Paul's Cathedral added to the oppressive discomfort.

On the platform, Reinhard Bonnke challenged Hindus to cast aside their gods and idols and accept the Living God. His shirt was stained with perspiration and his hair was plastered to his scalp and forehead as if he had just stepped out of a shower. A certain foreboding tugged at his heart, but he pushed it aside for the moment. He was not going to be intimidated in the city called the "goddess of death." He was here to proclaim *life*, and nothing would stop him, not heat, humidity, nor evil spirits.

He had arrived in Calcutta after attending a Full Gospel Business Men's Fellowship International conference in Singapore. Reluctant to go to Calcutta, he had been persuaded to visit his sister. When he arrived, he found that instead of a four-day family visit, a four-day Gospel rally had been arranged. Unable to refuse the opportunity to cast out the Gospel net, he agreed to preach.

The four days of furious preaching stirred the city of nine million people to shake off some of its squalid and pitiful character as Jesus came alive to thousands of Hindus. A minister of one of the city's leading churches said, "It is many years since I have seen so many people respond to the call to accept Jesus. This is the first time I have seen any evangelist challenge the people to break away from their superstitious trinkets that our people wear."

Reinhard's brother-in-law estimated, conservatively, that some four thousand souls repeated the sinners' prayer during the four days. Some sensational healings also were witnessed. One young girl's eyesight was restored instantly, and a middle-aged man who had been stricken with polio, testified that strength and healing had been restored to his legs. Those testimonies were multiplied many times over. Each night, crowds of up to two thousand struggled and jostled one another in the healing lines.

Another remarkable fact about this mini-crusade was the weather. It was as hot, muggy, and humid as a sauna bath, but the expected rains held off. It had rained right up until the day before the meetings and began to rain again when the final meeting closed. In fact, a deluge caught the car on the way to the airport, almost causing Reinhard to miss his flight to Johannesburg.

Disaster in Cape Town

On May 6, as Reinhard stood in the humid heat of Calcutta and began the victorious four-day meeting, the CFAN team and thousands of Christians some ten thousand miles away on the southern tip of Africa descended into a chasm of despair. A wind, seemingly charged with the fury of hell, blasted across the flats at Cape Town. In that wild, frenzy of destruction, the Big Tent was ripped and torn into a hundred pieces as if it had been run through a giant paper shredder. Shockwaves went around the world. The Big Tent, less than six months old, had been totally destroyed. More than a million prayers and a million dollars were swept away by a wicked wind.

Vicious storms had been battering the Cape for the past several weeks, hindering the erection of the massive tent for the forthcoming crusade. Seasonal rains earlier than usual had made the preparation of the site and the sinking of the giant steel anchors difficult, but the hard-working crew had stuck doggedly to the task.

The towering steel masts were eventually hoisted, and the huge roof panels were raised to form the majestic cathedral on a field next to the Cape Town suburb of Valhalla. Although wet weather had caused delays, the real concern was the wind. The Cape Flats are exactly that — flat as a giant table — and are swept even on calm days by ocean winds from the Atlantic. The technicians had been confident, however, when the site was chosen. After all, wind tunnel tests had proved the tent could brave winds of more than seventy-five miles an hour.

Even so, foreman Kobus de Lange could not help casting an anxious eye up at the roof seven stories overhead as the winds buffeted it and tugged at the steel cables. On May 5, a few tears had appeared in the roof fabric, but these were repaired, and by late afternoon, the crew was satisfied nothing serious would come of those minor rips.

By suppertime, however, it was obvious that the weather was continuing to deteriorate. The crew finished eating and wandered back to their sleeping quarters situated on the western side of the Big Tent. Some of the technicians decided to make some further checks on the cream and red structure which creaked and swayed as a fresh and strengthening wind buffeted the panels facing the southeast.

Gerhard Ganske, a tough, sun-bronzed West German who was in charge of the anchor system, slowly circled the perimeter of the giant structure, checking the steel anchors which were concreted into the soft, sandy ground of Valhalla Park. He had been confident they would withstand any known wind force. The steel cables, finely tensioned, pulled taut as stronger gusts of wind blew across the open field.

Milton Kasselman, the chief electrician who was to die tragically in a truck accident in Zambia some sixteen months later, walked inside the tent whose size was still breathtaking to the crew. Wooden benches balanced on tubular frames and arranged in thousands of rows gave off the smell of a large lumber yard. Kasselman stared up at the high-vaulted ceiling of fiberglass impregnated with silicon rubber and at the seven-story steel masts which appeared to sway gently in the wind.

His concern was for the lighting and sound system that he had been responsible for mounting and wiring up with miles of electric cable along with numerous control panels and switchboxes. Attached to seven masts and at strategic points near the platform were ninety-five floodlamps, each costing $1,200 and all securely mounted. Except for the occasional slap of cables against the material, Milton was hardly aware of any wind inside the tent. The design was such that air was funneled upward so there was no danger of wind slipping under the dome to build up pressure and whisk it away like an umbrella.

Tentmaster De Lange and his West German understudy from Stuttgart, Horst Kossanke (also tragically killed sixteen months later in the accident), made an overall inspection of the tent. Technically, all seemed fine. The anchor system, the steel masts, and the cables were a hundred percent stable. The only area that could not be checked, of course, was the actual fabric, but experts had assured them it would stand up to gale-force winds. They believed the repairs made that afternoon were more than adequate.

Sleep came easily to most of the team that night in spite of the violent gusts of wind and the bright arc lights that flooded the grounds as a safety precaution. The area where the tent was situated is notorious for its criminal element and few people venture out after dark, especially on a Saturday night.

CFAN security guards quietly patrolled in and around the tent and camp site. Midnight came and passed, and there were no intruders — although noise from nearby houses told of several loud and drunken parties going on. The temperature began to drop, however, and masses of black clouds skidded across the sky. In the distance, the dark outline of Table Mountain disappeared under a mantle of mist and fog.

About 4:15 a.m., some of the sleeping men began to stir in their beds. Outside the wind had risen to a constant roar. The trailers rocked to and fro, and everyone's thoughts flashed to the tent. Kasselman peeped out of his window and saw the tent seemingly still okay, and De Lange also looked to see that all was well. He decided, nevertheless, to get dressed and go outside to make a personal inspection.

Suddenly, above the roar and moaning of the wind, came another sharp sound — similar to a whip cracking — and an odd slapping sound, like material flapping in the wind. Security guards came running and within moments the camp was a beehive of activity with people jerking on whatever clothes were at hand

and running out into the cold blast of the early morning. All the anchors were still secured, but the once sharp silhouette of the profile of the tent was broken. A panel was beginning to tear and flapped wildly in the wind.

At first, De Lange and engineer Tony Bath were not too perturbed, thinking it was merely a repetition of the previous day and repairs could be made as soon as daylight came. Still, something pulled at De Lange's heart, and he decided to phone one of the crusade committee members in Cape Town and ask him to alert some of the committee to pray. He also decided to make a phone call to Johannesburg to one of the consulting engineers who had worked on the project and ask for advice. By 7:30 a.m., the rips were getting longer and more frequent. De Lange was virtually keeping an open line to the Johannesburg engineer, Stan Hughes, giving him a detailed report.

Shocked and bewildered, the crew stared at one another. The unthinkable was happening before their eyes. The material of the tent was being peeled off like a banana skin. Their first thoughts, of course, were to do something — but what? The wind speed at ground level was moderate to strong, but the velocity at the top of the masts would be far greater. It was impossible for a man to climb the masts. Even if he could, what could he do? The huge panels were being shredded into smaller pieces.

The appalling truth began to sink in. There was nothing they could do, except watch the systematic destruction of the world's largest Gospel tent. By about 9:30 a.m. when a watery sun probed the swirling clouds, the devastation was almost complete. The proud tent was gone. In its place stood a bare skeleton of steel masts and cables. Remnants of material clung defiantly to the supports in some places, but most of the twenty-two tons of roofing were now fluttering through the streets and gardens of Valhalla.

Team members wept unashamedly. Nearly five years of work dashed and destroyed in less than five hours. It was unbelievable. Smashed floodlights hung drunkenly from the masts. Amazingly, the loud speakers had suffered minor damage. Even more surprising was the fact that the two miles of timber seating had remained intact. For a few brief moments, they had feared the wind would begin to lift these and fling them around in the air. Mercifully, that potential danger was somehow averted. The anger of the winds, so it seemed, had been to deliberately savage the tent covering.

That was an hour of naked dejection for the CFAN team. While thoughts of what to do moved through the almost numbed minds of the crew, another group also was reeling under the dramatic reports of destruction. These men were members of the crusade executive committee, who had been responsible for the detailed organizing of the outreach. For nine long and hard months, a dedicated and devoted group, they had been praying and working for the Great Cape Town Crusade. Some three hundred pastors and church leaders had bonded together in an unprecedented unity to work for the success of the crusade.

A total of five thousand counselors had been trained by CFAN with another two thousand trained by local churches. Fifteen hundred ushers had been recruited and drilled in how to cope with the crowds.

Another sixty volunteer office workers had been busy night and day preparing the administrative back-up needed for such a large meeting. Now the committee began to ask questions about the future of the entire crusade.

At Valhalla Park, the wind began to subside and a crowd of curiosity seekers descended on the sports field around the stripped tent. Some laughed and jested. From the early morning hours, people had stood at windows and balconies in high-rise buildings and lined a nearby bridge, fascinated by the destruction. Photographers arrived at the scene and a full-color picture of the destruction blazed across the front page of a Cape Town daily newspaper the next morning.

Among the people who began to pour into the area, however, were hundreds of Christians. Throughout the day, believers from all over the Cape peninsula made a pilgrimage to the camp site. Hundreds knelt on the grass and prayed as tears flowed openly. A CFAN staff member commented, "It is like a funeral." Out of the prayers and tears came a wave of love and comfort which rolled over the hard-pressed team, who had been trying desperately to reach Reinhard in Calcutta and general manager Peter Vandenberg on a business trip to America. Unable to make contact with top management, they had felt very alone and almost deserted. In the middle of it all, however, the voice of God was about to be heard.

Encouragement From the Lord

Chris Lodewyk, head of the crusade committee who would soon join CFAN in a full-time capacity, was still in bed when De Lange called him about 5 a.m. that fateful day. An ordained minister, he had been for some years a champion for colored people's political rights until the Lord led him out of that arena. He had been on the planning committees for the Billy Graham crusade in South Africa in the 1970s and involved in planning other major conferences. He was not too concerned after the first couple of calls. He says, "I checked the weather and was comforted by the fact that the wind did not appear to be too bad. I believed the CFAN tech team would have everything under control." But at 9:30 a.m. when he heard De Lange bluntly say the tent was being torn up, he realized the seriousness of the situation.

He then drove out to the scene. "I was shocked as I came over a bridge and got my first view of the scene. I could not believe it. The tent roof looked like big flags waving in tatters from the masts. When I reached the site, I saw CFAN team members holding their heads and crying and weeping as they wandered around almost in a daze.

"The whole scene was depressing, and the noise of the flapping fabric and the whining of the wind through steel cables added a hellish dimension to the whole thing. In addition to the eerie noise, the ground all around the tent was vibrating like a continuous earth tremor," he recalls.

Immense pressure was being exerted on the masts and cables by the wind's wild flaying at the fabric, and the massive anchors were heaving and pitching, causing earth movements all around the perimeter of the structure. Once the crew realized there was nothing to be done to save the roof, they busied themselves trying to strengthen the steel work and cables and keep the grounds clear in case the masts collapsed. They, however, stood firm and became a silent testimony to the grace of God.

Although the wind that struck the tent was ferocious, many locals even today are puzzled by the fact that wind speed at ground level was not as strong as Capetownians sometimes experience. Lodewyk says:

"There are times when one has to hang onto lamp posts to avoid being blown over, but the wind that day was not nearly that violent. Yet when I looked up at those masts, I still remember seeing sinister black clouds swirling around. You could see that up in the air the wind was really strong. Like many others who were there that day and experienced the storm, I believe what we witnessed was undoubtedly satanic in its origin."

Lodewyk called an emergency meeting for that night, and the twenty-some committee members walked into the board room at the Lighthouse Church in Parow, they were wrapped in a cloak of depression. He could see a dead look in the eyes of his colleagues. "It is going to be a dry, dull, and sad meeting," he thought, "like pronouncing the final rites over a victim." The meeting meandered along for about five minutes, when suddenly one of the men stood up and began to prophecy. The board room became charged with a holy presence. The words were:

"My glory shall be the canopy that covers the people, and the praises of my people shall be the pillars."

Not one of them doubted that this was a command from the very throne of God. To a man, they were convinced that God Himself had spoken through His servant. From the depths of self-pity and despair, they were lifted up and a sparkle returned to their eyes and joy to their wounded spirits. The transformation was amazing, almost like an Upper Room experience. Immediately they made two decisions: the crusade must go on, and it must be at the present site. The meeting broke up with the room echoing with words of joy and victory.

But the battle was not yet won. There was still the weather. May is notoriously wet in Cape Town, and the cold Antarctic winds make outdoor meetings very uncomfortable, especially at night. So the crusade committee sent very specific messages to the prayer chains linked throughout the peninsula — pray for dry, warm weather.

It was the following day before news of the disaster reached Reinhard in Calcutta. As Reinhard boarded the plane on his homeward bound trip, his thoughts were focused on Cape Town and the Big Tent. He had a lot of questions on his mind: How serious was the damage? What would he do about the proposed campaign? What about the vision for the Big Tent? His battle cry, "From Cape Town to Cairo," seemed to have a dull ring about it with the flagship of his vision crippled and wrecked on the Cape Flats.

When the urgent message had reached him to phone his secretary, he said, "I knew in a moment that there was trouble with the Big Tent. In the same moment, I had peace. The Lord assured me that all was well." His first concern had been for any injuries. No one had been hurt, but his secretary tearfully conveyed the dreadful news about the tent. He hung up the phone, turned to his sister and her husband, and simply said, "The tent is destroyed."

His sister, Felicia, recalls, "There was no anxiety, no anger, no real sadness. His attitude amazed us. He seemed to have a calmness and serenity about him. He had instant peace in his spirit and knew that God was in control of the entire situation."

Thinking back, Reinhard confesses that the peace that filled his heart and mind was overwhelming. "When I lay down to sleep that night, I said, 'Lord, I'm worried because I'm not worried!' "

As usual, however, with anything God calls a person to do that is out of the ordinary, some of the harshest criticism came from other Christians. Some had expressed doubts about the project during the five years of its construction. Even when the tent was finished and in operation these critics continued to hound him, so — as unbelievable as it seems — when the tent was destroyed, these people rejoiced! They said it was the judgment of God. Others declared there must be "sin in the camp." Still others claimed God had blown down the tent because Anni Bonnke had recently cut her hair!

None of this ever affected Reinhard, although sometimes it got to the CFAN team who would find themselves doubting the wisdom of building the tent and of planning a grand assault on Africa. Reinhard, however, never doubted the commission from God to build the tent and to take the Gospel to Africa. His dedication remained unswerving even when the Big Tent and the large transport fleet ate up money faster than a Las Vegas one-armed bandit!

When he stepped into the foyer of the Witfield office, about fifteen of the staff who were not involved in the Cape Town crusade burst into song. To the strains of "We're together again, just praising the Lord," Reinhard and the staff linked hands, and a tear or two came into his eyes. Soon the tears were replaced by a holy fire as he shared his heart with the staff. All doubts were swept away immediately. The word "tragedy" was cast out and an air of triumph took over as he boldly declared, "This is just the start. The devil has overstepped his mark again. I know in my heart that something fantastic is coming. This ministry walks on miracles." There was no retreating. The vision was clear, and the passion to carry the Gospel from Cape Town to Cairo for Jesus was even greater. He would not cower or hang his head in despair with Jesus at his side.

10

A CANOPY OF GOD'S GLORY

When Reinhard had been told of the committee's decision, he had concurred immediately. On the way from the airport to the park, he turned to Chris Lodewyk and asked about the weather. Lodewyk, beaming from ear to ear, replied, "Don't worry. We have already provided the weather bureau with the report for the next two weeks!" Reinhard laughed and the boldness of faith rose in his heart. Yes, it was true. They walked on miracles, and no hurricane or demonic attack could stop the divine mission to see Africa saved for Jesus.

Arriving at the tent site, however, he was brought sharply down to earth as he surveyed the stark steel masts poking nakedly up toward the sky and the piles of ripped-up fabric rolled up and bundled together on the ground. Inwardly disappointed, he showed little negativity on the outside, and his usual faith and determination rubbed off on the team, who reconciled themselves to the fact of the disaster and began to believe that victory was still possible after all.

One of the stalwarts in the invisible spiritual battle was Suzette Hattingh, a one-time nurse supervisor who had been miraculously returned to full health after almost dying. Suzette, head of CFAN's intercessory ministry, led daily prayer groups throughout the peninsula. She had developed a powerful prayer ministry and, driving herself almost to physical exhaustion, she exhorted and sometimes bullied Christians to engage in intense warfare. Her prayer meetings are never dull.

No Wednesday night social visit with coffee and cake afterwards for her! She wears out the royal carpet to the Holy of Holies, pleading, interceding, and smashing down the strongholds of Satan that try to block the way. During those thirteen days before the crusade opened, she charged up thousands of Christians to pray and believe for a miracle in the weather.

And a miracle it had to be. Every Christian involved clung to the promise of the prophecy that had come forth at the board meeting. Other "words" of encouragement flowed at the prayer meetings, and a genuine spirit of expectancy prevailed. Cape Town, however, was not the only place where spiritual battles were being waged. The news had spread countrywide, and caller after caller kept the Witfield exchange busy with messages of comfort and strength. Around the country, pastors and ministries began to pray and intercede after the first shock and the tears were over.

A lot of concern, of course, was for the replacement of the tent. Was it insured? Was it possible to replace it soon? Reinhard assured his prayer partners that the tent was fully insured and that a replacement would be shipped out from America within months. Vandenberg, in America at the time, had preliminary talks with the manufacturers and insurance brokers, who gave a positive indication that the million-dollar claim would be met. This helped boost morale at the time, although later it was discovered that the claim was far more involved. Even at the time this book is being published, the CFAN claims have not been settled.

Many locals scoffed at the folly of the announcements that the meeting was to go ahead, come rain, wind, or cold. After all, who would sit in soaking rain and wind in nearly zero temperatures? Critics predicted failure for the crusade. Each morning at 5 a.m., Suzette and her loyal and devoted team rose to pray. Each morning, however, as they looked out through the curtains, the same grey, wet scene met their eyes. The weather, it seemed, got worse. In fact, the storms that battered the Cape the week before the crusade were described as "the worst in living memory."

On the day the crusade was to begin, the skies still looked like a watery sponge, but by afternoon a few patches of blue began to show in the grey heavens. By midday, rain had ceased around the park — although rain was reported only a few miles away. Yet it stayed dry at the crusade site. That miracle was reproduced night after night and day after day. Not one day after the meeting started was there not some blue "canopy" over the Valhalla Park sports ground. The weather had changed abruptly.

Warm air filtered in for the next three weeks, and the Cape Peninsula basked under the most gloriously warm and sunny skies. Puzzled weather experts described it as an "Indian summer." On only one evening was there a slight drizzle which actually came as a grateful relief, because hundreds of thousands of feet and thousands of vehicles had pulverized the ground into a fine, powdery dust which rose in great clouds around the sports field.

That first afternoon as the sun peeped through the grey skies, people began to arrive in dribbles which soon became a stream. By 3 p.m., the stream of people was a flood. Buses jostled through the congested traffic all afternoon bringing crowds to attend, and by the time Reinhard took the microphone, most of the wooden benches were filled. First-day estimates were put at twenty-five thousand people. A spirit of joy and praise filled their hearts. The Lord had honored His Word. This was undoubtedly going to be a great crusade demonstrating the glory of the Lord to the people of Cape Town.

By the third night when the crowds reached an estimated forty thousand, the ushers and security team were almost thankful not to be confined by the tent which could only seat thirty-four thousand under its canopy. The second Sunday produced an attendance of sixty thousand, yet God was going to do better than that. On the third Sunday, which was to have been the final day of the meeting, some seventy-three thousand people attended. At that point, it seemed impossible to close, so Reinhard extended the crusade by three more days. The final night, God shoe-horned in a crowd of seventy-five thousand!

Response to altar calls during those nineteen days had been listed at twenty-nine thousand. The impact was tremendous. Cape Town was gripped by "Jesus fever." People who had been too terrified to put a foot in Valhalla came to see what was happening. The suburb's nickname among locals was "Kill-Me-Quick" because of its dreadful record for crime and death. Yet during the duration of the crusade, not a single case of violent crime was reported to the police. Several senior police officers, puzzled by the sudden and dramatic drop in the crime rate, came to see for themselves the impact the Gospel was having on the people.

Everywhere the love of God gripped the hearts of the people. Whole rows of houses became Christian homes overnight as neighbors brought neighbors to the crusade and saw friends and relatives saved. Mighty waves of healing flowed through the crowd as well. One man from the reserved area, where people were so ill as to be carried in on mattresses, was so overwhelmed by his healing that he refused a seat. He spent the rest of the service walking up and down lost in wonder and awe. The feelings of the crowds at the miracles erupted into "the pillars of praise under a canopy of God's glory." At times, the platform resembled a hospital workshop, cluttered with wheel chairs and crutches, and with walking sticks decorating the front railings.

Reports of criminals and gangsters coming to Christ were a daily occurrence, and knives, revolvers, blunt instruments, and piles of stolen property were turned in by those who found new life in Jesus.

A young Moslem couple on a traditional journey to Mecca, the holy city of Islam, attended the meeting hoping to get Reinhard to give them a blessing on their pilgrimage! Instead, they found Jesus in a glorious way and announced they were canceling their trip to Mecca and going to Jerusalem instead. From the time the CFAN team first arrived at Cape Town, the Moslem community had taken a keen interest, visiting the site and engaging in debates with the Christians. When the tent canopy was destroyed, some unsubstantiated stories began to circulate that Moslems had marched around the site and called down a curse on it. This has never been proven. What *is* a fact is that many Malay people, who make up a high percentage of those who follow Islam, accepted Christ.

Several new churches were pioneered in the wake of the crusade, and already established churches bulged at the seams as hundreds of new converts were absorbed. For weeks afterwards, local pastors spent more time in baptismal fonts than behind the pulpits.

The Vision Is Raised to a Higher Level

In spite of the obvious victory of the crusade, the loss of the Big Tent was a great blow to the ministry's 1984 plans. After the official dedication, the first full crusade had been planned for Cape Town as the first step in the implementation of Reinhard's vision: "From Cape Town to Cairo." Plans had been to next pitch the tent at Durban and then in Pretoria, both in South Africa. After that the Big Tent was to move into Zimbabwe, Zambia, Malawi, and East Africa.

These plans were dashed by the loss of the canopy, although at first, there were hopes that a new tent roof could be delivered within a few, short months. It soon became apparent, however, that the insurance claim was only going to be settled after a long drawn-out process of investigation and possible litigation. In the end, the loss did not seriously hamper the great planned outreach. In fact, it catapulted Reinhard into a new dimension of evangelism that would reach masses of people he had scarcely believed possible. He still believes the Big Tent is part of God's strategy for winning Africa, but he readily admits that when the tent roof disappeared, God lifted his vision to a much higher level.

Even in the first dedication crusade, the crowds had overflowed the tent seating, and the people attending the Cape Town meeting would never have fitted into the tent. As soon as it had been erected, in fact, it already seemed too small! The Big Tent's seating capacity had allowed for adequate and wide walkways as specified by fire authorities. By reducing the walkways, they hoped to be able to add enough benches to raise the seating from thirty-four thousand to forty thousand. Extra loudspeakers were planned so people could hear, even if they could not get a seat.

The large crowds mobbing the Cape Town meeting had struck a chord in Reinhard's heart. The people of Africa indeed had become hungry for the Gospel. They would come by the thousands to meetings, he believed, even if it took a miracle to change the weather. He decided to embark on open-air crusades.

There was still the small yellow tent which had been used for years in rural crusades, but it was totally inadequate for the giant city-wide meetings which he envisioned. The smaller tent continued to be used in rural districts during 1984 and part of 1985, but its days were numbered.

The decision to go for open-air meetings apparently had the stamp of Heaven's approval for it moved the entire ministry into a new and dynamic role that would truly shake the continent. Reinhard's schedule remained as hectic as usual, both in southern Africa and abroad. There was some debate whether or not to continue with Durban and Pretoria as planned, but the pull northwards was getting ever stronger. A small rally was planned for Bulawayo, Zimbabwe's second largest city, in early October, with a second larger crusade set later that month for Harare, the nation's capital and largest city.

The thought of establishing a permanent base there had not entered their minds. The Great Harare Crusade, however, would not only confirm the decision to hold mass outdoor meetings, it would dramatically change the team's entire outlook and cause an upheaval in many of their lives.

Harare Breakthrough

Reinhard actually had been champing at the bit to move north since before the dedication day for the tent. Someone asked him how he felt then, and he said, "You know, I don't care much for all this ceremony. I just want to get on the road and go north. That is what is burning inside of me."

Then, after the Soweto dedication crusade, he wrote to his prayer partners: "The voice of the Holy Spirit is calling us across the Limpopo River. Yes, we will move into Zimbabwe later this year. Harare is the target city, and together with God's people there, we will throw out the Gospel net."

The meeting in Bulawayo was held as sort of a warm-up, and the results were outstanding as people flooded onto the hired soccer field and sat under a blazing sun. Their umbrellas made a colorful scene in the middle of the parched, brown grass. A total of fifty thousand people attended with almost ten thousand registering decisions for the Lord. Again, the meeting was punctuated by some remarkable healings.

The planning and organizing of Chris Lodewyk and the intercessory ministry of Suzette Hattingh were the backbone of the crusade. A chain of more than twenty-five hundred prayer warriors was built up with four prayer sessions a day. The meetings began on this sure foundation of prayer, and the praying became even more intense once the crusade started. To the casual passerby, the noise coming from the prayer hall was like the deafening scream of a jumbo jet. Inside, people were spreadeagled on the floor moaning and praying. Others "wailed" against the walls, while some knelt silently and still others walked or strode around in a wide circle. Some of the warriors clasped their hands; others waved their arms in the air like baseball umpires. The seeming scene of bedlam and chaos, however, was in reality quite the opposite. There was no confusion in the minds of those praying; they were engaged in the most deadly of all warfares — pressing against the gates of Hell.

The people praying came from all walks of life: women with babies strapped on their backs, a father carrying a young child while a four-year-old clung onto his jacket as he paced, a grey-haired white woman clutching her handbag in one hand and a Bible in the other. A pair of nuns, far away from their convent's cloistered silence, gamely indulged in earnest prayer, although some apprehension showed occasionally at the boisterous outbursts from some of the men who physically punched at the air as they prayed. Amazingly, there was never so much as a whimper from the babies.

This facet of the ministry largely goes unnoticed in the multi-thousand crowds, the drama of the huge altar calls, and the signs and wonders which follow. The victories demonstrated in the stadiums and large crusades, however, are planned and executed in the realm of prayer. Here, unseen by the masses, the real battles are fought and won. From the prayer halls, the power of God is released to bring about the success of the crusades — all to the glory of God.

At one of these prayer sessions, however, something inexplicable happened. Suddenly one of the elderly men who had been a devoted member of the intercessory group slumped to the ground and died. For him, it must have been like falling through a window into the very presence of God. For Suzette and the others, it was a challenge. How dare the devil come and pluck away one of their dear brothers! That was a purely human reaction to the shock of sudden death with no one being able for the moment to consider that maybe this brother had run his course and was more than content to become part of the clouds of heavenly witnesses. They prayed, praised, and exhorted for five hours trying to bring about his return from the dead.

Then they had to allow him to rest in peace and call the police — who asked some awkward questions about why the group had waited so long to call them. It took quite a lot of explaining to pacify the authorities, who were hardly impressed with the explanation, "We are Christians, and we pray for the dead to return to their bodies." It was a great praise session, those five hours, but later they had to laugh at themselves for storming Heaven without first asking the Lord whether He wanted such a storm in this case.

Nightly, the Harare showgrounds became the gathering place for thousands. On the final Saturday, as the meeting was in progress, a fine drizzle of rain began which soon became a sharp downpour, sending several hundred people scurrying for shelter. Most of them sat it out in the open, however, enjoying the much-needed rain. At first, it looked like a passing shower, but the rain persisted and conditions became quite difficult for those on the platform.

Huddled under umbrellas, the crusade committee held an emergency meeting and had it very much in their minds to close the service and hope for a sunny afternoon the next day. Then a few voices raised in the plea, "We want the Gospel," became staccato shouts and then a general chant from thousands of throats. Reinhard grabbed the microphone and began to preach the good news. As the rain came down harder and the faithful thousands sat drenched to the skin on the long lines of wooden benches, he preached harder. The message was on the Holy Spirit and hundreds received the baptism and the sound of many tongues filled the rain-drenched air.

The next afternoon indeed brought nice weather, and the final meeting was held with the rainbow vista of umbrellas protecting colorful clothes from the brilliant sunshine instead of the previous day's rain. The total crowd estimate for the entire crusade reached three hundred thousand during the sixteen days, with a total of thirty-one thousand decision cards completed.

One elderly lady, who had arrived at the crusade blind and walking with great difficulty, was among those healed. She said that when hands were laid on her, she felt a sudden warmth and blinked her eyes. At first, she saw what looked like distant stars, then suddenly the harsh glare of the floodlights struck her pupils. She could hardly be restrained as she tried to get to the microphone and tell the crowd what had happened. She traveled almost fifty miles north to her village the next day and told the people what God had done. Within hours, she was having her own revival.

A few days later, a CFAN video team and photographer visited the village to see the revival for themselves. The entire village of about one hundred and fifty people turned out for a church service. The local school teacher confirmed that the woman had been blind for ten years. Not only was her sight restored, but that morning she danced for joy in the middle of the village to demonstrate that her leg disability also had been healed.

In a newsletter sent out the week after the crusade, Reinhard reported on the tremendous results and related that one hundred and thirty-eight churches representing thirty-eight denominations supported the meeting. "The level of unity was high, and this is the key to a mighty sweep of the power of God," he wrote.

A couple of months later, a popular Zimbabwe magazine ran a feature article headlined, "Who Are the Holy Crusaders?" Generally, the article had a positive tone, although it did make mention of the fact that "some major churches were not invited — the Roman Catholic and Methodists among them — and others declined because of the Pentecostal teachings of CFAN." The writer then made these interesting observations:

"It was, therefore, surprising to discover that Roman Catholic nuns, as well as members of other faiths, attended the CFAN activities. It was even more surprising when some of these people responded to the altar calls.

"When the 'miracle-working' Pastor Bonnke took the pulpit, it marked the beginning of experiences that had to be seen to be believed. The new converts were challenged to break away from all superstitions — including ancestral worship — and even a witchdoctor discarded the tools of his trade, which were burnt. At one stage the rostrum resembled a 'rubbish dump' as hundreds of converts threw away all sorts of items from packets of cigarettes to lucky charms and bracelets."

The magazine staff also spent some time following up and investigating some of the healing reports. It was interesting to read the confirmations of these reported in a secular magazine.

After the crusade, Reinhard said prophetically, "In 1985, we will move farther into Africa, pressing on until the whole continent echoes to the name of Jesus. May God open our eyes to the things that are imperishable." He is a visionary, and although he shares his thoughts with his colleagues, it is sometimes hard for him to understand why it takes so long to cause the visions to become reality. As the Lord has enlarged his capacity to dare bigger and grander things, he sometimes grows impatient with the mundane, day-to-day functions necessary in a ministry the size of his that has to operate with a minimum of personnel. He will not allow his team to shy away from finding ways around any obstacle which arises. CFAN is not a ministry for weak-kneed Christians.

A Brush With Death

A young British couple, who had come to Zimbabwe especially to experience a major crusade, were caught up in tragedy shortly after the crusade and experienced what amounted to a really close brush with death. They were staying in the home of Mike and Roz Oman of Youth With a Mission near Harare when they heard a crash outside. Two vehicles, one driven by a personal aide of Prime Minister Robert Mugabe, had been involved in a collision at an intersection.

The young couple, Gordon and Rachel Hickson, ran to try to help the injured people, along with Mike Oman, while Roz telephoned for help. While they were trying to pry open doors and drag passengers out of the vehicles with the aid of a young doctor who was passing by, an Army truck came along and rammed into them. Three of the "good Samaritans" were pinned against the car wreck, while Mike just managed to scramble away, although his lower leg was briefly trapped under the moving wreck.

The driver of the army truck jumped out and ran. Both of Rachel's legs were smashed. Gordon had a fractured pelvis, and the doctor had been grotesquely impaled by a heavy steel crowbar they had been using to pry open a car door in the first wreck. Fortunately, another medical doctor stopped to check out the injured and supervised their removal by unskilled ambulance personnel who arrived in about fifteen minutes.

Prayer immediately began to go up for the three, especially during the surgery that followed. The crowbar, that had entered one side of his chest and exited just above the hip bone, was successfully removed from the young doctor who survived his dreadful experience. Rachel's life was in danger for some time, and the doctors gave her only a 5 percent chance of living. Even then, they felt she might suffer serious brain damage. To the doctors' surprise, however, she recovered completely after a lengthy convalescence in England — and much prayer intercession.

In fact, the power of prayer prevailed in the entire situation. The aide who had died in the crash had been a senior intelligence officer of the administration. When the news of the accident reached the highest authorities, one of Rachel's bedside visitors was Mrs. Sally Mugabe, who spoke quite openly about the Lord. Rachel and Gordon then received an entourage of top government officials, who got them flown quickly to England.

The Hicksons have returned to Africa with their daughter Nicola as part of the CFAN full-time staff. In spite of their grim ordeal, they believe God has called them to work in Africa. Their accident and what happened a year later are strong reminders that the saints are not immune from vicious onslaughts of the devil.

In the meantime, Reinhard's planning continued. The Harare success gave him further confidence to plan other outdoor meetings, and he looked forward to 1985 with relish at what the Lord would accomplish. He also looked forward to the For Inter-African Revival Evangelists (FIRE) Conference, which had been postponed in 1984, and was now set for October 1985. Lodewyk had been named conference director and given the mountainous job of putting together the international event, which was expected to draw more than four thousand delegates.

11
THE IRON GATES OF ISLAM

Early in 1985, Reinhard decided it was important to launch deeper into the continent, and a reconnaissance into West Africa was made. He and Peter Vandenberg visited several West African nations, including the Ivory Coast, Togo (where they met with the President), Ghana, and Nigeria. In Nigeria, they visited Benin City, where Archbishop Dr. Benson Idahosa has his headquarters.

Reinhard had met Idahosa, a mighty apostle and evangelist in his nation, many years before, but this was the first meeting of significance between the two men. Idahosa, who studied at Christ for the Nations Institute in Dallas, has been responsible for the planting of more than two thousand churches in his country. He is seen from time to time on the three major Christian networks in the United States.

Both men are of international stature but have very different styles. Reinhard preaches the Gospel, then prays for the sick. Idahosa preaches healing first, and then the Gospel. Both achieve remarkable results to the glory of God. To the casual onlooker, Benson Idahosa appears a little overpowering at times, especially in the traditional, flowing Nigerian robes which make his six-foot-one figure even more noticable.

The vision for Africa's salvation is nothing new to the Archbishop, but to hear it again from the lips of this German evangelist thrilled his soul. In turn, he opened up his heart, and what he shared touched

Reinhard deeply. Idahosa was planning a crusade in the Nigerian city of Ibadan, a Moslem stronghold. Usually as brave and courageous as an African buffalo, he was approaching the proposed crusade with more than a little trepidation. He had been to the city, and it was a hard city, a city where Islam is entrenched. He had never experienced any real spiritual breakthrough in Ibadan. Would Reinhard combine forces with him for a week's crusade?

Reinhard remembers, "At that moment, the Holy Spirit touched my heart, and I responded to my brother's plea. We agreed to share the crusade costs, although I knew that CFAN's purse was empty. Deep in my heart, however, I knew this was the perfect will of God. So we agreed to share the burden and the ministry."

Only one week in their schedules for the year was open for both men, and that was only four weeks away. Could a crusade be put together in such a short time? Both felt so strongly that this was God's doing that they agreed on the dates, and Idahosa immediately rushed his huge organization into top speed.

On the flight back to their base, Reinhard and Peter had time to reflect on the consequences of what they had done. Their share of the crusade costs would come to about $100,000, and both knew it was actually going to be a struggle to meet salaries for the next month, much less another crusade budget. Still, Reinhard had the inner assurance that he had acted in pure faith, that there was no possibility of presumption.

Within a few days of returning home, he received a trans-Atlantic telephone call from a California millionaire who had become a personal friend and taken some of CFAN's ministry affairs in America under his wing. A mild-mannered, unassuming business-man, Barry Hon has a great love for the Lord's work and does not waste words. The Lord had impressed him there was an urgent financial need at CFAN, and a check for $40,000 already was on the way. The Ibadan crusade would go ahead.

Nigeria is a nation of some one hundred and twenty million people. In fact, one of every four persons on the African continent is a Nigerian! The visit to Ibadan, however, was a very different experience for many of the team. Time has stood still in the market place. There are no neon lights or supermarkets with pushcarts. Instead, the housewives barter and haggle over prices, while customers have every opportunity to see the goods at close quarters, whether they are fruit, vegetables, or fresh meat.

With a population nearing four million people, Ibadan is reputed to be the largest city south of the Sahara. It is an old city with a myriad of small buildings spreading for many miles. In times past, it was a major trading center with the Arabs, who traveled down from the north. Early Portuguese traders also paid periodic visits to Ibadan. The Arabic influence is still felt with 50 percent of the population followers of Islam. The other 50 percent is made up of Christians and pagans.

The lifestyle of these people is simple, and there is overcrowding and a lack of basic essentials. A newspaper article about that time admitted that only 33.3 percent of the houses had water and only 56 percent had electricity. Despite their material lack, the people proved to be open, friendly, and wonderfully receptive to the Gospel.

Reinhard's staff and Idahosa's entourage met with a most unusual welcome. Arriving at the airport, they stepped onto the landing field to be met by a glittering array of army and police officials. Reinhard was escorted to a shiny Mercedes and found himself the head of a motor cavalcade which snaked through the old and often dingy city. He smiled and waved to the crowd in the best American electioneering style, even trying to shake a few hands along the way. But this was not his style. He felt uncomfortable, especially with the obvious and striking contrasts of wealth and poverty.

He was soon gripped, however, by the atmosphere in the city. Hope and faith were in the air. Idahosa and his workers had done a first-class job of publicizing the meetings, even buying time on the local television station. The people were well-informed about the meeting where two of the world's most dynamic Christian speakers would share the platform.

They came by the tens of thousands to the Olubadan Stadium. The local newspaper estimated one crowd at half a million. Conservative estimates by crusade organizers, however, cut that down to a quarter of a million. Nevertheless, it was the largest crowd Bonnke had ever preached to before. At the first meeting, the crowds gave them a traditional welcome by taking out handkerchiefs and waving them gaily in the air. During the entire crusade, Reinhard adjusted to local customs and wore a traditional Nigerian robe, which he called his "garment of praise."

Only those who came early were able to get seats in the grandstand, but the crowds apparently were oblivious to time or the inconvenience of standing on the open field. The meetings were truly anointed by the Holy Spirit and were constantly interrupted by explosions of excitement from the crowd as people realized they had been healed by the power of God. They stood for hours, singing and praising and worshiping the Lord. It was impossible to keep an account of the miracles. The local newspaper gave extensive coverage to the crusade, even reporting many of the miracles and including photographs of some who had been healed.

The size of the crowds staggered even the local media. One story read, "Never in the history of the Nigerian Federation have people gathered in such large numbers for such an occasion. Not even the visit of Queen Elizabeth of Great Britain to Nigeria or the historic Independence Day or any political rally has attracted such an indescribable meeting of heads for a single purpose — to be healed and recreated."

One day the crowd was so large that traffic police were unable to control the congestion. Two officers collapsed from heat exhaustion as they battled to direct traffic at intersections. People and vehicles blocked every street for two miles around the stadium. Police told organizers they had turned away at least thirty thousand people. Among those trapped at one point was Idahosa, who leaped out of his vehicle and began to direct traffic.

The secular newspaper exhibited tremendous freedom to report the crusade, unlike most of its counterparts in the Western world. The reporter, obviously a Christian himself, even boldly commented on the theory of evolution. He wrote:

"Words of God are hard to believe, for some. There are millions who, instead of tracing their origin to God, claim their origin from the ape. I don't belong to that school of thought and neither do Nigerians. What is happening in the state capital is the redeeming hand of the Lord, working to remove our poverty, unhappiness, and other ills of our way."

Summing up the Ibadan experience, Reinhard said, "In all the years of my ministry, I have never seen what I experienced there. What this crusade has done to my own heart is not difficult to imagine. We at CFAN are moving out and into the heart of Africa to capture this mighty harvest for the Kingdom of God. Hundreds of thousands of people have heard the Word of God in this crusade. I have been deeply moved. God is fulfilling His Word. We will take the continent for Jesus from Cape Town to Cairo. A mighty wave of faith and power is sweeping over Africa as the Holy Spirit does His marvelous work."

Winning Australian Hearts

A country which has taken Reinhard to its heart is Australia. The Christian media have given his African campaigns wide coverage, so it was no surprise when he was asked to speak at the 32nd World Convention of the Full Gospel Business Men's Fellowship International, held in Melbourne in March 1985. This convention followed closely after the Ibadan crusade, and Reinhard was fired up with a new drive and enthusiasm. His stories of the Nigerian crusade held the crowds spellbound.

His dynamic preaching caught the eye of the secular press, and an entire page was devoted in a local newspaper to an article on his ministry. The article included five action photographs of him as well as one of the dramatic crowd scenes from Ibadan.

The article read:

"Each night rallies were held in the huge Melbourne Sports and Entertainment Centre. It reputedly holds about 8,000 and was full every night. On the last night of the convention, it was standing room only. Officials estimated the crowd at more than 10,000. The big drawcard for the night rallies was a quietly spoken (at least when you meet him face-to-face) German evangelist by the name of Reinhard Bonnke.

"Pastor Reinhard Bonnke is one of the world's leading evangelists, and in terms of sheer numbers converted, probably the world's most successful in the past ten years. His home ground is Africa, where he is literally turning that continent upside down. And watching and listening to him in Melbourne, it is not difficult to understand that sort of result. His delivery is electrifying. His voice whispers one moment, then rolls like thunder, rocking the cavernous hall the next. During the Melbourne rallies at least 500 people went forward to be saved each night, with more than a thousand the final night." (Excerpt from a John Gagliardi article, *Townsville Bulletin*, March 1985.)

Interestingly enough, another writer was at the conference observing Reinhard's style and impact. He was Owen Salter, the editor of an independent Australian national Christian magazine which treads warily when it comes to the Charismatic/Pentecostal movement. Yet the magazine writers and editors have a keen appreciation of those movements' places in the Kingdom of God. Salter's comments, published several months later, come from a man with an "orthodox" Christian background. Under the headline, "Rompin' and Stompin' for Jesus," Salter wrote:

"Reinhard Bonnke's preaching style wouldn't suit the normal parish pulpit. It wouldn't be big enough. Bonnke likes to stride around the stage, bend down low, throw his arms up into the air like a triumphant boxer. He's celebrating victory — the victory of Jesus.

"Even when he is hoarse with laryngitis and speaking through a cranked up PA, his thickly accented German-English accent has a penetrating quality. He is the only man I have heard who could shout in a whisper. And shout he does. It is one of his more common voice modulations. But Bonnke leaves even the most enthusiastic American evangelist for dead. The best I have ever heard from the Land of the Eagle was a big black preacher named E.V. Hill, whose delivery never dropped below 100 decibels. Bonnke used a wider voice range and moved like an India rubber man with it.

"I encountered Bonnke in action on the stage of the Melbourne Entertainment Centre . . . it was a remarkable experience. He preached for over half an hour, then invited people to come forward to receive Jesus or to be prayed for regarding healing or deliverance from spiritual affliction.

"It was a receptive audience — Charismatic brothers and sisters from around the world, along with a large number of local Christians. Go forward they did. No doubt there were even some non-Christians in their number. But what happened next was totally unexpected. As he instructed those still in their seats to pray, he told the people who had come forward that a commitment to Jesus was all or nothing. It meant a complete break with their old lives.

"So far, so good. But then he said, 'I'm going to get you to throw onto the stage your cigarettes, your alcohol, your occult objects, and I'm going to stomp on them in the name of Jesus!' Stomp on them? In the name of Jesus? Wait, I thought, wait and see. An appeal for alcohol and occult objects at a world convention of the FGBMFI seemed to me a little, well, hopeful. Perhaps he had failed to make the mental transition from non-Christian African crowds to an Australian Christian audience, I reasoned. I was prepared to allow him the possibility of a few cigarettes.

"Then an even more unexpected thing happened. He pointed to a part of the crowd to his left and said, 'God is telling me someone down here has an occult object. He wants you to throw it up onto the stage now!' Nothing happened. Then, after a few seconds, someone threw up a packet of cigarettes — from the outside of the crowd. Unfazed, Bonnke strode across (the stage) exhorting his audience to unite their praises for victory while he proceeded to stomp on those cigarettes in the name of Jesus.

"Not just polite little steppings-on, not even a vigorous grinding under the heel, but a full-blooded, both-feet-off-the-ground jump that saw him landing on that cigarette packet with enough force to break a brick. The poor thing never had a chance. But Bonnke wasn't finished yet. He continued stomping as other items, unrecognizable from my position on the balcony, were thrown under his feet. Then he walked across the stage. 'God is still telling me that someone here has an occult object to get rid of,' he said. A second or so went by.

And then, just as he expected, up it came. Bonnke stomped with joy.

"I admit my reactions as I left the Centre were mixed. I categorized the experience as a culture-shock — a little piece of Africa had found its way to Melbourne, and I had been unprepared for it. No doubt back across the Indian Ocean, Bonnke's approach is perfectly appropriate. Yet despite my discomfort, I found myself admiring a man who was prepared to go out on a limb, to stick to what he sensed God was telling him, even if he ran the risk of looking a fool. Moreover, I was sure, despite my scruples, that people had done real business with God. I had little doubt that some had been freed from bondage to smoking and to the occult. I believed this because I knew that such liberation comes because God's power locks in behind faith — whatever outward expression that faith might take.

"I had the chance to interview Bonnke, and I asked him if he experiences the same enthusiastic response in Western countries as he does in Africa.

" 'No,' he admitted, 'I believe the reason for this is that God's harvest fields are not all ripe at the same time. It seems to me that there is a rotation in this matter, and I believe that this is God's hour for Africa.'

"Is there, then, something that makes Africans more in tune with God's Spirit?

" 'Africans do seem to find it easier to put their trust in Jesus,' he said. 'They hear the Word, put their faith in it, and it happens.'

"Well, what stops it happening in the West?

" 'I believe the origin of our unbelief is Western education. At great expense and effort, it reshapes our minds in the opposite direction to the Word of God. Then we say we cannot believe in something that can't be proved — like the Word of God.'

"Yet Bonnke still insists God is capable of breaking down Western prejudices. One way, he believes, is through trusting Him for 'signs and wonders.' 'It's as old as the Acts of the Apostles, it's the ministry of Jesus. It's simply a matter of returning to the original pattern. The idea — often expressed to me by Westerners — that it's a question of mentality is utter nonsense and I resent it.

" 'I was preaching last year in Zurich and right in the front row was a lady who had been confined to a wheelchair for 20 years. I was preaching — I hadn't prayed at all for the sick yet — and suddenly she stood up. She was walking and crying! Lots of people present knew her and her illness, and those people went nuts! The stiff Swiss! No, it's not a question of mentality. When God moves, people move, no matter what culture.

" 'If God's people are bold enough to speak in line with the Word of God, God proves His own Word. None of us needs to defend the Almighty. A lion needs no defense. Just open the cage!'

"I had seen enough to know that (Bonnke) was basically right. I wanted to tell myself it's easier said than done, but I couldn't help feeling . . . well . . . uncomfortable. Again. But this time, not about the style of a visiting Bible-thumper. I was finding out how disconcerting it can be to come face to face with a man who takes God absolutely seriously. In the end, returning to the 'original pattern' of the early church has to be an all-or-nothing exercise . . . ." (Excerpts from *On Being*, November 1985.)

Return to Zambia

In August 1985, CFAN moved to Lusaka, the capital of Zambia, for a crusade. The meetings had been scheduled for evenings, but because of security restrictions, they had to be held in the daytime. Despite the awkward hour of 2 p.m., it seemed many thousands of people somehow got off work in the afternoon to attend. Two hours later, people would still be arriving, although Reinhard would be almost halfway through preaching. Time stands still in Africa for most people. Deadlines and keeping up with the clock are for Westerners. Watches are not timepieces, but items of jewelry.

Here, demonic manifestations marked the services right from its first day and continued through the final Saturday. Evil powers would manifest causing people to leap up and start wailing or writhing. Ushers would rush in to carry out the afflicted person. Often it would take four grown men to carry out one demon-possessed woman. Tremendous violence would be manifested in these people as Christians attempted to cast out the evil spirits. It was a common sight to see a counselor sitting on someone's legs while two others held down the person's arms and prayed for them. Still, the victims would twist and buck, tossing their heads from side to side and contorting their faces in gruesome gestures with glazed or wild and defiant eyes.

Because the influence of witchcraft is still very common and because most women — even in a capital city like Lusaka — go to a witchdoctor for any personal illness or when a child gets sick, some 99 percent of the possessed victims were women. Marriage problems also result in visits to a witchdoctor. The men, who work in towns and cities, tend to give more credence to conventional medical care but make little or no attempt to stop the women from going to witchdoctors. Many women were set free, but many others found it hard to believe that Jesus could set them free and keep them free from evil spirits. This strong witchdoctor influence also means children are brought up in an aura of witchcraft coupled with worship of ancestral spirits. These influences are powerful forces that bind millions of people in Africa.

Reinhard became so accustomed to the demonic outbursts that he was hardly perturbed by the rushing of ushers into the crowd to get to another possessed person. Even the crowd was calm, hanging on to his every word and somehow sensing that today they would find the truth which would set them free from all the satanic influence, obviously such a part of everyday life.

Many people not attending the crusades were not so friendly. One morning, four staff members of CFAN went to the local market to get some photographs and see what foods were offered. Markets in Africa are much the same — smelly, full of flies, and rather unhygienic. Open sewers wind between mud and grass structures with dingy interiors and crooked wooden shelves on which a pathetic few tins of tobacco, stale-looking sweets, or bundles of candles are precariously balanced. Within a few minutes of arriving and taking a few photographs, however, the visitors were scolded by some self-appointed market marshals, who destroyed their film and hustled them out of the market.

A Zambian television crew arrived on the last day to shoot film for a documentary on CFAN. Heading the crew was a man who had accepted Jesus during the 1981 Lusaka crusade in the old yellow tent. It was a thrill to meet him and know that the fruit of 1981's crusade was still flourishing. The motto of Zambia is "One Zambia, One Nation." In fact, after the five-month campaign in 1981, the slogan might have been "One Zambia, One Savior — Jesus." The campaign had covered Livingstone, Kabwe, Ndola, Kitwe, as well as the capital, Lusaka. That first crusade in Zambia not only extended Reinhard's vision but gave the team practical experience in conducting campaigns of such length so far from home base, a thing that has become common in the years since.

I had flown to Lusaka to report on the closing four days of the crusade and then travel by road with the crew to Lubumbashi. There was a tingle at the back of my neck as I arrived in the land of my spiritual birth. Twenty-four years previously, I had accepted Jesus in the copper-mining town of Mufulira in Zambia, then had pastored Calvary Tabernacle in Lusaka for almost three years. Later, I had gone back into the newspaper business until joining CFAN in 1982 as editor and publicist.

The morning after the second crusade closed, the trailers were hitched up, the huge left-hand drive Mecurius Deutz motors roared, and the convoy started sorting itself out on the road through Zambia to Zaire. Hundreds of Christians lined the road to bless and cheer us on as the CFAN team set out to challenge another stronghold of Satan.

167

12

ON THE ROAD TO ZAIRE

As the vehicles edged across the sports field, kicking up dry, brown grass and clouds of dust, it seemed a pity to be leaving so soon. The response of the Zambian people had been so wonderful and joyful that it was hard not to stay on and preach, but the task of caring for the new Christians and carrying on the Gospel thrust had to be left in the hands of the local churches.

One of the most commonly asked questions by the ministry's partners around the world is, "What is one of the mass crusades really like?" Even those who attend a crusade rarely get a look at all the work that goes into putting on one of the meetings. Each crusade, of course, brings its own problems as well as its own blessings. The trip to Zaire, however, was unusual in several ways, so perhaps it is a good one to show some of the behind-the-scenes aspects.

The convoy — one minibus, three small closed trucks, three travel trailers, one car, and five beautiful red and white tractor-trailer rigs — moved out onto the Great North Road at 9 a.m. that beautiful, sunny Sunday. Ahead lay a drive of two hundred and sixty miles. That night was to be spent in Chingola, and on Monday — after another forty-two mile drive — the Zaire border would be reached. Once clear of the border, plans were to reach the crusade city, Lubumbashi, by lunchtime.

It was a new experience for me, driving in a massive 18-wheeler, especially a left-hand drive vehicle. (In South Africa, we follow British driving customs and drive on the right, usually in right-hand drive vehicles.) I soon realized that I had to be the "eyes" for Don Preen, who was driving, when it came to overtaking slower moving traffic. Trying to calculate the speeds of on-coming vehicles and just how much time and space we needed to get past another vehicle was something I found rather hazardous. Don and I began to work as a team, piloting our giant rig along the highways and along the tiny byways of some towns. I will never know how we did not take a set of traffic lights with us when we cut a corner a little sharp in the town of Ndola that afternoon!

Trips through Zambia are always slow because of road checks. The police are looking for gangs smuggling in hard-to-get foodstuffs (mainly luxury items) and drugs. Zambia, unfortunately, is a dropping-off point for a major drug-peddling ring operating between India, Zambia, and South Africa. The convoy reached Chingola, however, by 5 p.m. and parked on a sandy vacant lot almost in the middle of the main shopping area. Chingola is a mining town. The nearby Nchanga mines are the richest copper ore-bearing mines in the world. The convoy formed a rough square reminiscent of the covered wagons in old American Western movies, and the drivers then took stock of the situation.

A stroll the length and breadth of the main street revealed no public toilets and certainly no shower facilities. Fortunately, a local pastor arrived and took the three women in the party to his home for a hot bath. For the seventeen men, however, there was not even a washbasin, much less a shower. After supper cooked over a big campfire built right in the middle of the square under the open, starry sky, we found a cold water spigot in one corner of the vacant lot. So I marched off with soap, towel, toothbrush, and tooth paste. It was rather an odd faucet, set in the ground at ankle level, with a dubiously dark drain beneath it and tall grass growing around. At least it was water and, hopefully, fairly clean. For a person who had spent most of his life in the city and was accustomed to chrome and tile bathrooms, this was really living rough!

Four of us who had not driven during the day agreed to take two-hour guard shifts. We slept in a steel section of one of the tractor-trailers which had been fitted up with bunks and steel hanging cupboards. About the best thing that can be said for that sleeping arrangement is that one can lie down! The bunks are hard, the mattresses are thin and rustle when anyone turns over, and someone always snores. That night, the steel doors closed with metallic "clungs" whenever the shifts changed, and icy drafts seeped in through the air vents. The trailers usually are left hooked up to the cabs, and one person sleeps in the driver's bunk — causing the dormitory container behind to sway as though in a heaving Atlantic swell every time the driver turns over. The crew members who take these convoys of equipment from one crusade to another deserve a lot of credit.

Magnanimously, I had volunteered to do the "dogwatch" from 4 a.m. to 6 a.m., but I had not taken into consideration the fact that I would not be able to go to sleep by 11 p.m. The unaccustomed and uncomfortable bunk and the noises of men snoring and turning over — and doors opening and closing for those on the earlier watches — finally caused me to give up the idea of sleep and do the only useful thing I could, which was pray. About 3:30 a.m., I gave up even trying to rest and relieved Kevin Royston early. It was extremely cool as I paced around the shadowy outline of our fleet of vehicles. Several guard dogs were tied up on free-running chains at each end of the camp. It occurred to me the dogs might mistake me for an intruder since I did not usually travel with the convoy. Also, I was all wrapped up and brandishing a heavy wooden stick. I decided to give them a wide berth and patrol the outer perimeter of the camp, but I need not have worried — the dogs were fast asleep. I wondered who was guarding whom!

As the first tinges of red stained the sky, I wondered how I was going to make it that day. I had not slept in more than twenty-four hours but consoled myself with the thought that we would be in Lubumbashi within a few short hours. Little did I realize what a long and harrowing day lay ahead. The joy of the Lord was in my heart, however, and that meant He would strengthen me. And He did. After a breakfast of hot cereal and a slice or two of plain bread, by 7 a.m. we were winding our way through the early morning traffic and out onto the main road, heading for Zaire. Although we were on the road again, very shortly we had to make another stop. In a situation such as this one where sanitary facilities are not available, there has to be a stop as soon as plenty of open bush becomes available. Traveling in Africa usually is under the most primitive conditions.

After successfully clearing several more road blocks, the convoy crossed the border and was met by Pastor Ronald Monot, a life-long missionary to that country who was organizing the crusade. He was at the border to interpret because very little English is spoken in Zaire. The main languages are French and Swahili. Also, he provided sleeping accommodations for the ministry team and Reinhard at his own home.

The convoy attracted a flock of children who had to be restrained from climbing all over the vehicles. They took a special delight in teasing the guard dogs traveling in a special steel-netted cage on the back of one of the small trucks. The weather grew hotter and stickier while the multiple pieces of paper were cleared by customs and all the passports stamped. Just after clearing the border post, there was another police check point where Pastor Monot had to give a long explanation of who we were and what we were going to do. So it was 2:20 p.m. when we reached the town.

Lubumbashi gained world notoriety in the early 1960s as Elizabethville, the stronghold of Moise Tshombe, who had employed a private army of mercenaries to help him gain independence for the province of Katanga. Once a cosmopolitan city, it had been well-patronized by rich white miners from Zambia (then Northern Rhodesia). When Belgium granted independence to Zaire and pulled out almost overnight, the nation was plunged into chaos and anarchy. In the ruthless struggle for control of the country, some of the worst fighting and gravest atrocities occurred in and around Elizabethville.

As the convoy drove through the city twenty-five years later, stark reminders of that bloody civil war still remained. Buildings burned out during the fighting still stood as desolate black shells. A mile-long brick wall was pock-marked with bullet holes, as were some of the walls of buildings. The traces of war were not as striking, however, as two other things: the swamp-colored minibus taxis that carried unbelievable numbers of people and the hordes of children that ran and danced along the pavement as the long convoy edged through the streets — acting almost as if a circus had come to town.

Before the CFAN crew could begin to set up on the crusade site, the central customs and immigration offices had to be visited with more formalities to be gone through and papers to be checked. As the vehicles waited on the street, continuous droves of children passed. These children were very adept at picking pockets and snatching any item left unguarded, as one of the crew found out the hard way when he lost a sweater slung over the seat behind him. We discovered the hordes of children in the streets were a result of two things: a school holiday and the fact that the country's birthrate during the past few years has skyrocketed. Children now make up more than 35 percent of the city's seven hundred and fifty thousand population.

Most of the green taxis were at least fifteen years old and looked as if they belonged in a junkyard. The convoy often looked like an island in a moving junk heap of green metal. Windshields were cracked, fenders buckled or non-existent, and each had some welding patches showing on the bodywork. Shock absorbers had long since worn out. Sometimes the "passengers" included live chickens, and at times, a taxi passed with a passenger hanging on a side door, just content to be riding home and not walking.

The tall towers of the banked floodlights of the stadium came into view, and after some twisting and turning, the convoy drove through some rusty corrugated iron gates and into the sports grounds. On the right was the stadium, ringed by an embankment of concrete seats and a steep, covered grandstand under which were the offices and locker rooms. Moving onto an adjacent practice field, the crew began the task of trying to set up a proper, livable camp for the next seven days. Later, we found that a lot of people — particularly the children — usually spent a large part of their days playing soccer on the fields where the convoy was parked. So we were setting up camp in the middle of "their" territory.

The stadium was in a residential area opposite a large open-air market. Within half an hour of parking, the convoy was surrounded by a thousand or more young children who unmercifully teased the guard dogs and threatened to overrun the camp, if given the opportunity. The loud chattering and giggling began to touch a few raw nerves among the crew, already exhausted and haggard from two long and tiresome days of driving and a night of not very comfortable sleep.

Our first concern, however, was to look at the bathrooms. As there seemed at first sight to be plenty of facilities for the public, the crew was optimistic. When we neared the grandstand, however, an awful stench began to reach our noses. The reality was actually worse than the smell with urine and excretion plastered over toilets, washbasins, floors, and walls. It looked as if it would take weeks to clean the place. We found, however, that the main gates to the offices and the team rooms under the grandstand were securely locked, so there was every chance those facilities were clean, especially as an international soccer match against Kenya was scheduled for the Sunday after the crusade.

Meanwhile, the children were becoming more hostile, and it was decided to let the dogs loose. The man in charge of the Alsatians was sure he could call them back before anyone actually was hurt. The idea was simply to scare the children into backing off a little way. The tactic seemed to work at first. When the children saw the dogs were being loosed, they turned and fled. On command, the Alsatians returned — but so did the children! Then it became a game to see how far they could get into the camp before the dogs were set on them.

A local Christian brother tried to make his way through the throng of children to welcome CFAN to Lubumbashi. Unfortunately, he got caught in the middle of a dog charge, and his leg was injured. One of the drivers had to run to his rescue. Then a crew member's young son, helping unload, fell and badly wrenched his knee. In addition to the children on the field, the twelve-foot-high wall near the convoy was now ringed with additional hundreds of children whose legs dangled over the wall as they kept up an incessant commentary in French and Swahili. Nerves were beginning to reach the breaking point, even among the team. The frustration of not being able to communicate with the children aggravated the situation. It was almost sundown, however, and we hoped they would soon leave the area in peace.

In the meantime, a key was found to the team locker rooms under the stadium. Hopes soon fell as we found no electric lights — the bulbs had been stolen out of the sockets — and a sickly stale smell permeating the locker rooms. The water had been turned off, and the toilets and urinals had not been flushed for weeks. They were filthy but not as bad as those outside. The showers had been used as a toilet, and a swarm of mosquitoes descended as soon as the door was opened. The locker rooms had become a huge incubator for millions of mosquitoes. Two of the showers were usable, but needed to be scrubbed of dried, soapy dirt, dead insects, a squashed frog, and other unidentifiable grime.

I commandeered two local men who worked in the stadium and used sign language to get them to bring buckets and a hose. Scrubbing brushes, soap, and disinfectant were available in the trucks. The rest of the team was busy unloading, and I found that I was now the self-appointed health officer in charge of toilets and showers. It was the dirtiest job I had ever undertaken. I was kept going only by the thought of a warm shower to clean off the grime of two days on the road. After pouring ammonia everywhere and almost suffocating myself with insect spray, I found there was no hot water! Cold-water showers were the best that could be had. The floors and walls were now clean, however, and it was a breath of Heaven to smell the freshness of soap and water on my skin again. I was beginning to get a perception of crusade life in Africa!

After a good dinner came another shock — guard duty again. No hero, this time I volunteered for the first stint, from 9 p.m. to 11 p.m. Also, my complaints about sleeping conditions brought an offer from Gerry Davies to share the cab with him. Home, for the next seven days, was to be the cab of that truck. I finished my guard duty sleep-walking and was asleep as soon as my head hit the pillow.

The next morning, the crew decided it was impossible to leave the CFAN camp in the present location because of the security risk posed by the children, especially when the camp was unoccupied during services. The best and most secure spot would be inside the main stadium at the back of the goal posts. The entire arena was ringed by a high barbed-wire fence. Tentmaster Korbus De Lange was concerned that Reinhard would be unhappy about finding the camp in the middle of the stadium, but hoped he would understand once the advantages were explained.

So the trucks, trailers, and other vehicles were moved. The next major task was to get the lighting, sound system, and platform rigged. The first meeting was scheduled for 3 p.m. the next afternoon. Local churches cooperating in the crusade provided plenty of help with the work, but the language barrier again proved a problem. It also was a searingly hot day with a blustery wind that kicked up dust and dry grass all through the day. Blue jeans were a pale shade of brown by evening, and blond hair ended up a reddish-brown color.

The children returned just after breakfast, but the barbed-wire fence kept them at bay, although quite a few dared to climb over it. Possibly they were lured on by the crew's washing, strung out on makeshift lines tied between the kitchen vehicle and one of the travel trailers. Several local Christian women came by each day to do the washing in big iron tubs out in the open. The temptation of the shirts, jeans, and shorts hanging on the line was just too much for some of the children, who braved the barbed wire *and* the guard dogs to attempt grabbing some item. The crew managed to protect its clothing and nothing valuable was taken.

Toward lunchtime, there must have been at least five thousand children on the stands, which remained the norm for the rest of the crusade. They stared and called "meester, meester" all day long. The noise of their shouting, cheering, and taunting was almost like that of a crowd at a soccer game. Later that day, when some of the youngsters added stone throwing to their tricks, one of the team became so fed up that he grabbed a child and turned him over his knee! That youngster got the shock of his life when he found his bottom well and truly tanned. Others among the CFAN group were upset, however, and pointed out that the ministry was there to show the love of God and preach the Gospel, not to correct the children. After some open debate and prayer, the differences were resolved and the incident buried.

To my delight, I found myself removed from guard duty. Now that we were behind fences, we were able to let the dogs run loose at night. However, I had to get used to sleeping in perpetual daylight. Because of security, floodlights blazed directly into the camp all night. Also, all night, a distant sound vibrated in the air, a moaning sound that sometimes sounded like singing. We did not mind this, however, after finding out the sound came from a group of women maintaining a twenty-four-hour prayer vigil in one of the rooms under the main grandstand. Those women were the unseen pillars for the crusade that was to begin.

When Reinhard and the ministry team arrived the next day, they were taken from the airport to meet with the city commissioner and other officials. Through an interpreter, the commissioner pointed out that Reinhard was following in some illustrious footsteps — Pope John Paul II had been a visitor to the city only a week earlier. In fact, one of the local newspapers had carried advertisements for the Pope and the CFAN crusade on facing pages.

The Crusade Begins

The first day of a crusade is always a thrill. By 2 p.m., people were beginning to arrive. An hour later, the huge covered stand on the west side was filled. The crowd soon overflowed onto the main playing field. Estimates put the numbers at seventy thousand. This crowd, however, was excitable and noisy, and Reinhard had great difficulty in "reaching" them. He preached one of his shortest sermons on record, prayed a general prayer for the sick, then asked for those touched by the Lord to come forward. What followed was chaos. People stampeded toward the platform. Among them were some who had been healed, but others simply wanted to get to the platform for a personal "blessing" from Reinhard — probably a carryover from the Pope's visit. The situation became almost dangerous as the mob began to crush up against the platform, including women and small children.

The platform became a place of refuge with the sick, lame, *and* healed trying to escape the surging, pressing crowd. The team began to pull up children who were being crushed against the tent poles. After a few testimonies, Reinhard decided to dismiss the crowd. It had been impossible to control the altar call and get people to counselors. The meeting broke up in general disarray. Nevertheless, the Gospel had been preached, and many miracles of salvation and healing had taken place.

That evening, Reinhard, his general manager, some team members, and some local people met to see what could be done to handle the crowds. This was the first time in CFAN history that crowd control had completely failed. The local people said we should have a row of policemen in front of the platform assisted by ushers, who would help people with genuine testimonies get to Reinhard on the podium. No CFAN member was anxious to have uniformed policemen on duty, but it seemed this was the only form of discipline to which the people would respond. Police were very much in evidence throughout the city. One could hardly travel a single block without encountering them stopping cars and checking for personal tax clearances, overloading, and licenses. Overloading, the most common offense, apparently was taken care of by a few bank notes passed swiftly and silently from hand to hand. Scant attention was paid to the road worthiness of vehicles, otherwise the transport system of the city would have ground to a permanent halt.

Apparently it is a case of "when in Rome," for even the Christians there operated according to local police customs. Once during that week some of the crew suffered the misfortune of being stopped by the police, who demanded to see the driver's license. Explanations were difficult, and after much handwaving, it became obvious the officer was going to insist on *seeing* the license — which, unfortunately, was back at the CFAN camp. Someone else's license was offered, but the policeman became louder and more officious. Fortunately, Pastor Monot arrived on the scene with a small attache case under his arm in which he usually carried a bulky supply of banknotes. A brief consultation, and we were waved on. Monot's attache case had saved the day!

For the rest of the crusade, a platoon of policemen took up positions each day in front of the platform. Crowd control then became possible, although the follow-up program for new converts had to be abandoned because of the huge numbers who responded. Also, street numbers for homes in many parts of the city did not exist, so there was no way to get addresses.

The second night, the crowd numbered only about fifty thousand, but there were some outstanding testimonies of the sovereign move of God. Reinhard was more relaxed as he preached a bold message, tough on sin. The tent crew hoped some of the thousands of children among the crowd would hear the message! They continued to be unruly, sometimes throwing sand or handfuls of grass, and constantly talking and laughing.

Rains were not due for another six weeks, and the playing field was losing a lot of grass. The children's scuffling raised clouds of dust, which created quite a problem for the sound man. At the close of the service when the people began dancing and praising the Lord, his booth, which was right in the middle of the crowd, would practically disappear from sight as he frantically tried to protect his equipment from the fine, red dust.

No attempt was made on the second day to have a full-fledged altar call. Those wanting to accept Jesus were asked to raise their hands and repeat the sinner's prayer where they stood. We hoped that Christians sitting nearby would make contact to establish fellowship with the new converts. That was an unsatisfactory method, but at this crusade, the new converts had to be left to the Holy Spirit as Comforter and Guide.

Testimonies of healing could have gone on all night, however. The impact of the crusade, even under difficult circumstances, was reaching into every corner of the city. Zaire Television then requested permission to do a direct broadcast from the stadium. A direct radio broadcast also was planned. In addition, the television producer, a Christian, wanted to have Reinhard and other team members on a panel discussion one night during the week. The Lord was opening every possible door to get the Gospel spread abroad in Zaire.

An incident during the third service illustrates the necessity of spiritual discernment when ministering in Africa. When Reinhard asked those who knew they had been touched by Jesus to come forward, a tall, sharp-featured woman neatly dressed in a traditional long caftan came through the crowd. Her arms were raised as if she was praising the Lord. The crowd began to applaud, but Reinhard boldly spoke into the microphone that she was under the control of an evil spirit. Some of the team stopped her from getting to the platform, and immediately she became convulsed and began screaming. Ushers carried her away and prayed for her deliverance. The woman could have thrown the entire meeting into confusion if she had succeeded in getting to the microphone. In Africa, the preacher has to depend on the Holy Spirit, and not his deacons or elders, to filter out the troublemakers.

All the meetings had been scheduled during the afternoon because the authorities did not want the meetings to run late into the night. However the Saturday starting time was set later because the city commissioner had declared a "clean-up day." A curfew was set from 2 p.m. until 5 p.m. Anyone traveling during that time had to get a special police permit, otherwise his vehicle could be impounded, and he might find himself spending the weekend in jail. During those hours, residents were expected to clean the city pavements and streets.

That morning, a special staff meeting was held to discuss the impending move to Harare. The devotional time before the meeting. became, in hindsight, of considerable significance. General Manager Peter Vandenburg's theme that morning was sacrifice and the price each must be prepared to pay to follow Jesus. Normally a smiling and cheerful man, that day he was uncharacteristically tearful, and his voice choked as he asked, "Are we . . . am I . . . prepared to sacrifice my life?" It was a somber moment, but only a brief one, because people's minds usually dismiss thoughts of death with, "It won't happen to me." Yet two men in that crowded kitchen where the staff met were going to make the ultimate sacrifice in the cause of the Gospel within a few days.

Saturday was another searing hot day, but by 1:30 p.m., at least two hundred people were already sitting on the grass near the front of the platform. Most of them were elderly or sick. Some could not walk, others were blind or deaf. They were a pathetic sight, and the meeting was not to begin until 5 p.m. They sat in the scorching heat all afternoon, not moving or trying to find any shade. They had brought no food or water with them. We were deeply touched and actually hurt for people so desperate for good health that they were willing to sit for hours on hard, dusty ground in blazing heat to reach out to Jesus to make them whole. The crew carried them bottles of fresh water during the afternoon.

In spite of the obvious attractions of the local nightclubs, the stadium filled with a crowd of some fifty thousand once again that night. Reinhard kept the message short in order to give more time for testimonies, because it was obvious the number of healings was far exceeding anything we had seen in Lusaka. Faith was high. There was one note of discord, however, and again that came from the children. Because the meeting started later than usual, they had flooded the playing field and started several little soccer games among themselves. Most of the time, they did not even have a proper ball to kick around, only one made from old rags tightly bound together with string and twine. When the meeting began, repeated requests were made for them to stop playing, but to no avail. Neither the adults present nor the police did anything to control the children, who continued playing even after the sun went down because the floodlights were on.

So during the sermon, some four hundred children shouted, screamed, and dashed around the far side of the field, kicking up dust, and enjoying their game. I walked to the far side of the field, hoping to persuade the youngsters to show some respect while the message was preached, but they began the good-natured chant of "meester, meester," so I stopped. One little boy began to smooth the skin on my hand and forearm. A nearby adult understood some English and explained that the little boy "just wants to feel a white skin." Only then did it become obvious that we were such an oddity to the children because many of us were white. We discovered that of the seven hundred and fifty thousand people in Lubumbashi, only about three thousand are whites. The children were fascinated at watching the "rare birds." Some of them had never seen a white person before.

The closing meeting was a joyful occasion with dozens again charging up to the microphone to tell the crowd of about sixty thousand what Jesus had done for them. An elderly women arrived almost doubled over and hobbling on a stick, which she threw away before the cheering crowd and walked upright on the platform. Her joy overcame her when Reinhard took her hand, and the pair began dancing before the Lord.

In spite of the hassles, it was a week of vivid memories of great testimonies of the power of God. Many children were among those healed. Just one experience such as the twelve-year-old boy healed of a crippling hip condition made the long, hard journey seem more than worthwhile. He had not been able to run, jump, play sports, or even walk upright, yet as his mother told of his condition, he did a series of leaps into the air to show what Jesus had done for him. The joy of the mother and son was contagious. The meeting was televised "live" and for weeks exciting reports were heard of people watching by television who had been healed when Reinhard prayed for the sick. Many TV sets were on in the local hospitals throughout the province and some people were healed as they lay in hospital beds.

A crusade obviously takes a lot of hard labor on the part of the crew as well as the ministry team, to say nothing of the advertising and administrative work that goes on, plus the follow-up done by local churches and volunteers. In fact, working in a crusade is an ideal way for Christians to learn unity and to develop patience and love for one another. Not all crusades are as hard to run as this one, and hopefully, none of them in the future will be followed by the kind of tragedy that followed the one at Zaire.

13

TEARS OF JOY, TEARS OF SORROW

The camp siren sounded at 5 a.m. on Tuesday, a beautiful clear day. The air was crisp and clean as the crew washed in cold water and made ready to start the long haul back to Johannesburg and home. The day before had been spent taking things apart and packing the vehicles for the journey. Everyone was hard at work before breakfast stowing away the last few items and checking that the trailers were all coupled to the tractor cabs and ready to roll.

Before starting, the team gathered on the field just behind the goalposts, sang a chorus, then joined hands and prayed for a safe journey. Often there is a certain perfunctoriness attached to prayers for a safe journey. Somehow, many times the necessity for such a prayer seems abstract rather than real. I had the urge to add a prayer based on Psalm 91 to those already offered, feeling the prayers had not been powerful enough. Then the thought occurred that I was being vain, and before I could decide to go ahead and pray, the meeting broke up. As events unfolded later that day, I wondered in anguish whether obeying that little urgency to pray extra would have had any influence on circumstances. Since then, I have realized I will only know for sure when I see Jesus, so it would be foolish to get into condemnation. I doubt if I will ever pass up another such "urge," however.

After saying farewell to Pastor Monot and his wife, Sheila, and other local Christians, the convoy pulled out of the Mobutu Stadium headed back for Zambia. Grounds workers already were busy watering and trying to repair the surface of the field which had been badly damaged by the thousands of people attending the crusade. They would be hard put to get the field in shape by Sunday's international soccer game.

Despite the deterioration of some sections of the road where tar had been broken up completely and swept away, and in spite of being stopped at the usual police checks, we reached the border by 10 a.m. — then spent the next three hours patiently and meticulously going through all the necessary papers with the customs officials. The five tractor-trailers were supposed to set off in a pre-arranged order with the slowest one in the lead, but because of frustration at the border delay, each driver pulled out just as soon as he was allowed to leave. Gerhard Ganske's rig stayed in the lead, followed by Englishman Kim Fullam, Horst Kosannke with Milton Kasselman as his co-driver, Gerry Davies, and Friedhelm Wentland driving the last truck, followed by the ten-passenger minibus. I rode with Davies.

After another brief stop at a police check, the convoy really got rolling. The plan was to drive straight through and make Lusaka by midnight. I was standing outside the customs building when the first truck pulled away, and I ran across towards mine, passing in front of Kosannke as he swung the wheel around. Kasselman smilingly waved at me as I passed his side of the truck. It was the last time I saw either of them alive.

The road through Zambia was narrow but fully tarred. On each side of the road, tall grass waved back and forth from the wind caused by the slipstream of the trucks. Stretching out ahead of us were some huge slime dams from the nearby Konkola copper mine. During the rainy season, a lot of these tailings run off into the brush, then during the prolonged dry months, the debris breaks up into a fine, white, powdery dust. Sitting high up in the cab of the powerful vehicle, I felt absolutely secure as smaller cars and trucks passed us by. Davies and I, who had pulled out fourth in line instead of first as planned (because our rig was the slowest), were chatting away when suddenly we saw a heavy tractor-trailer approaching at high speed. Davies moved as far over to the side of the road as he could, then another rig passed us traveling as fast as the first. There was a terrific explosion right next to my ear, and we flinched then looked around in bewilderment. Finally, we realized the outside mirrors of the two vehicles must have touched.

I adjusted the mirror which, amazingly, was unbroken. Then I looked up to see still a third truck coming at us. Later, we found out that we had met a convoy of trucks carrying fuel from South Africa to Zaire. At that point, Psalm 91 was working overtime in my mind, and my knees were distinctly weak. The third oncoming driver, however, apparently had encountered the rest of our convoy and was aware of how narrow the road was. He was traveling with one wheel off the tar, leaving a good safety margin in the center of the road.

Unfortunately, his safety precaution caused an even greater hazard. The multiple wheels of the rig were billowing up dense clouds of fine, white dust, which a light breeze was blowing into the middle of the road. Davies had slowed down even more because of the passing trucks, so the vehicles ahead of us were no longer in sight. Visibility was greatly reduced because of the cloud of dust. The third oncoming truck passed safely, then we plunged into the dust trailing behind it.

Davies slowed down even more saying, "Man, this is dangerous. I must slow down."

He began to gear down and ease on the brakes. We were only in the dense cloud for a few seconds, but burst out into the bright sunlight to see a huge, red, cylindrical fuel tank lying just off the center of the road and about fifty yards ahead. To the right of it was a dark mass of metal. On the left and a few yards past was one of the CFAN trailers half off the road tilted at a steep angle.

Braking hard, Davies stopped. I yelled to him to switch on the emergency lights, half expecting to see our fifth truck coming out of the dust cloud and plowing into us. Then we ran to see what we could do to help. At first, we thought the drivers of the CFAN rig to the left had just pulled off to give assistance. As we ran towards the red fuel tank, diesel fuel was spilling out onto the road. The tank had been punctured on top also, and a fine jet of fuel was spurting skywards. Smoke and flames could be seen farther up the road, and small flames were licking around the base of the tank.

I turned to look at the dark, metallic mass that had baffled me and realized that it was a trailer and part of a truck. I gazed again at the red fuel tank, then suddenly noticed, lying in a pool of diesel fuel, the crumpled body of a black woman. Flames were beginning to run toward her. I had jumped out of the truck without shoes and now realized I had better get them on before trying to run into any flames. As I ran back down the road I saw Friedhelm Wentland, driver of our last rig, parked a safe distance behind us along with our people who had been in the minibus.

I yelled at Wentland to pick up the woman, and he and someone else placed her a safe distance away on the side of the road. We found later that she was a hitchhiker picked up by the driver of the fuel truck. By the time I had my shoes on, the rest of the men had dragged out all available fire extinguishers. One was shoved into my arms, and we all ran to the spot where the containers were being threatened by the spreading fire. Flames and great plumes of smoke were everywhere. As we battled through the tall, dry grass to get a side view of the CFAN trailer sitting there, the full horror of what had happened hit me.

The CFAN rig off to the left was completely engulfed by now in roaring flames that leaped high into the air, and neither driver was anywhere to be seen. There was no sign of life except for those of us just arriving. One of the crew tried to get closer to the fiery wreck with one of the extinguishers, an act of sheer desperation because the puny little extinguisher would have made no impression whatsoever. Even as he crawled forward, there was an explosion, possibly one of the tires. Three of the team stood back under the shadow of a giant anthill and began to wail and cry for their brothers in Christ.

For a moment or two, I stood paralyzed. What does a Christian do in a disaster situation like this? I began to pray in tongues because my mind certainly did not have the answer. Standing in the tall grass, I suddenly became aware of another danger. Flames were now spreading from the wreck into the dry grass, and diesel fuel was running down the road and into a gully alongside. Our truck and the one behind were in danger — as well as the minibus and all of us standing out on the road — of being trapped by a wall of flames on each side.

I rushed down from my vantage point and shouted to my colleagues to help divert the river of diesel fuel to the bush. As we attempted to divert the fuel so as to be free of fire on at least one side of the road, I glimpsed out of the corner of my eye the starkness of the tragedy in human terms. Rudi, the son of Horst Kosannke, the driver of the rig on fire, rushed past me screaming, "Where is my father? Where is my father?" I saw him a few moments later, wild-eyed and ripping his shirt in anguish. Still later, I found him sitting in the cab of one of our trucks, red-eyed and sobbing but also full of rage. I put an arm around him and prayed, although no human words are ever adequate in such a situation.

Outside, the flames seared the sky and sinister clouds of black smoke lifted high into the blue heavens, visible for many miles. From nowhere, hundreds of people, mainly children, had now appeared to chatter and watch the drama. By now, the rest of the convoy ahead of us had stopped, and some of them had returned. Shock and dismay were on all our faces. Grown men cried unashamedly. I remember walking along the side of the road with my arm around one of them. Although deeply grieved myself, the Word of the Lord came strongly into my heart, and it was simply this: To be absent from the body is to be present with the Lord. (2 Cor. 5:8.) I tried to comfort my colleagues and lift their spirits, but it was hard. All around us now was the smell of death.

That was the longest and most trying day of my life. The accident happened about 1:30 p.m., and it was ninety minutes before a fire truck from the mine arrived to douse the flames. Then came the gruesome task of trying to remove the bodies and piece together how the accident had occurred. There was an unpleasant scene when a member of the local Red Cross arrived, smelling heavily of alcohol, and began drunkenly to accuse us of smuggling ammunition. Several men on the CFAN team have quick tempers and, before they came to Christ, were quite capable of handling themselves well in a fight. It was an amazing act of grace that restrained them from flattening that official.

Also there were some over-officious actions by the police, who threatened me because I was taking photographs, mostly for insurance claim purposes. Then there were spectators pressing in on us, and one of our team members seemed to be only concerned with getting on to Lusaka. All in all, nerves became ragged and edgy from grief, frustration, and aggravation. In such tight corners, one finds out just how much the Word of God controls one's life!

Comfort in the Middle of Distress

In the middle of all the distress, the Lord provided comfort, strength, and practical help. Among the spectators was a group of Christian women who came to offer condolences and to pray. Then mine management officials arrived to offer assistance, and a local farmer and his sons brought boxes of soft drinks and offered the CFAN convoy refuge on their nearby farm that night.

After the wreckage was cleared from the road, which was closed all afternoon and held up all traffic between Zambia and Zaire, we went to the farmhouse on the banks of the Kafue River. Also among the group was Danie Kasselman, the younger brother of the other victim, Milton Kasselman. As we sat around a long table in the large courtyard of the farmhouse, with the Trytsman family preparing a huge chicken barbecue, we sang songs of praise and began to pray for the wives and families of Horst and Milton. The impact of the tragedy only then had really hit the team. The two victims were now with the Lord, but their wives and children were left behind to suffer loss and make the real sacrifices.

During the afternoon, De Lange had notified Reinhard of the tragedy, and he began trying to charter a plane to join the team as soon as possible. Nobody on earth will ever quite know what happened that afternoon. De Lange, out in front of the convoy, was the first to encounter the oncoming trucks. When he saw how fast they were traveling, he radioed back to some of the drivers who were equipped with walkie-talkies. One of the men he spoke to was Milton, warning him to beware of the fast-approaching northbound convoy. He called again a minute later and got no response, but thought maybe a small hill was hindering the reception. Only when he looked back in the rear view mirror and saw the first puffs of smoke did he realize something was wrong.

An inquest resulted in the cause of the accident being listed as "unknown," and no one was held responsible. Most of us, however, are sure that the cloud of white, powdery dust was the key cause. Based on what we saw and what was found out in subsequent insurance investigations, apparently Horst entered the cloud of dust and kept his rig on the extreme edge of the road. There was a slight embankment, however, and the truck apparently began to slide causing the rig to slightly jack-knife, which he probably tried to correct.

About the same time, a fourth oncoming truck entered the same dust cloud. That driver would not have had to wander over the center very much to have collided head-on with Horst, who was battling to control his own rig. That seems to be the best possible explanation. When the two rigs collided, the fuel tanks ruptured, and an electrical fire started immediately and soon became an inferno.

There is an unsolved mystery surrounding Milton Kasselman's death, however. His charred body was found stretched out next to the crumpled cab of Horst's rig with the only physical injury a broken wrist. A witness who arrived seconds after the impact says he saw him run around the rig and try to help the other man. Milton's widow, Jane, has a theory that her late husband fainted when he looked into the cab and saw the extent of Horst's injuries. She said he could not stand the sight of blood and would faint when one of the children suffered a small cut. So it would appear that he amazingly survived the impact, only to either be knocked out by the explosion or simply faint and then be burned to death.

I lay awake that night thinking that it is relatively easy to die for Jesus, to give your life in the cause of His Gospel, but had I ever really asked my wife and children if they were prepared for me to make that sacrifice? There is a sense of adventure for the men on the great Gospel crusades in Africa, but if sudden death comes as it had that afternoon, they would be transported into the presence of Jesus leaving a legacy of tears and anguish for their loved ones. Yet no other cause, no matter how noble it may sound, can compare with that of the Gospel. There is no greater honor than to live and die for Jesus.

As Chris Alberts drove Rudi Kosannke and myself to Lusaka Airport in the Toyota Corolla the next day, I could not help but notice that I involuntarily stiffened each time I saw a big truck hammering towards us. Chris also noticed a tendency in himself to ease off on the gas whenever we met a truck. Finally we realized we must not cower under any devilish deception of fear. I must confess, however, that each time I see a truck coming my way, I have an instant recall of September 3, 1985. I am not fearful when driving, but perhaps that scene is lodged in my memory to remind me of how frail we are — like the grass of the field, blooming one day and withered and blown away the next. (1 Pet. 1:24.)

Reinhard met up with the convoy just outside the town of Kitwe, and they all hugged and shed a few tears on the side of the road as they prayed and comforted one another. Speaking at the funeral a few days later, Reinhard recalled his thoughts as he sat in the back of the plane carrying the bodies of the two men back to Witfield:

"It was like carrying the bones of Joseph back to the Promised Land, not that there was anything special in the bones, but there was a promise with them. God would fulfill His Word. Yes, even over my own death and grave, God would fulfill His Word for Africa to be saved."

Also at the funeral, Reinhard recalled a warning given by the Holy Spirit some two years earlier:

"The Holy Spirit spoke repeatedly that a time would come when some of us would lay down our lives for the sake of the Gospel. The Holy Spirit spoke of martyrdom. The path we are treading is red with the blood of martyrs who have gone on before us. But no matter what the price or cost, this vision will find fulfillment. Even if we were to back out, God would find someone else. But we will go this way until the end, until Jesus comes. The blood of the martyrs is the seed of the Church. The more Satan kills the saints, the more God's people prosper, the more the Kingdom of God grows."

He made a direct challenge to all of the CFAN team at the funeral, "We are not backing out from this divine call. If anyone says he cannot pay the price or the road is too rough, I will ask him to rather look for a more comfortable ministry. The road ahead is tough and rough, but at the same time, glorious. I for one want to walk it to the end."

With such a challenge and the two coffins of our brothers in Christ before us with the South African and West German flags draped at the back of the podium, there was not one member of the CFAN ministry who could not say, "Amen," to the call to persevere.

The Zambia and Zaire crusades had been glorious events, but at what a price. Being involved in frontline crusade evangelism is not all "hallelujahs." The tears of joy can become tears of sorrow.

14

A CALL FROM THE EAST

A major departure from the crusade calendar in 1985 came when CFAN received a call from the Far East. They were invited to hold a full crusade in Singapore in December. Reinhard had visited Singapore on brief preaching engagements, and now the local Christians wanted him to return and stage a proper crusade. Although he has traveled the world and spoken on every continent, his big city crusades have been held only in Africa. Before the visit to the East, however, another major crusade was held in Africa, two visits were made to Great Britain, and a rally was held in Australia.

Ever since the Nigerian crusade, Reinhard had been eager to return to the populous West Coast where he sensed that God's harvest was ready to be reaped. So in October 1985, CFAN went to Accra, the capital of Ghana. Planning for the crusade had been initiated by CFAN organizer Ekkehard Homburg, assisted by local missionaries Frans and Esther Kleefeld, who later became CFAN representatives in West Africa. Some twenty-five churches and ministries joined in the Ghana Pentecostal Council which invited CFAN to hold the crusade.

Two days before leaving for Accra, Reinhard received a message that permission to use the stadium in the center of the city had been withdrawn. This is typical in Africa where decisions often are changed overnight by officials who take no thought of the planning and preparation that may have gone into an event.

As it was, thousands of posters and handbills had been handed out for the crusade, and Christians were eager that it proceed. The alternate location was an interesting one — the local race course.

When preparing a press release after the crusade, the CFAN publicist could not resist the following introduction: "In Revelation 19, we have the picture of the triumphant Lord Jesus Christ riding the white horse, and in Accra, the Savior was again the winner when CFAN held a giant crusade on the local race course!"

The change in location resulted in a slow start with only twenty thousand people attending the first evening meeting, but the power of God was evident. As the news spread through the city, attendance doubled each evening. On the final night, there was a crowd estimated at one hundred and twenty thousand people.

At the first service, five women testified of being healed of breast cancer; and, on the second night, a blind four-year-old received his sight. A little girl who had been unable to walk for seven years brought roars of applause when she began to jump up and down on the platform. The final service was held on Saturday morning at 8 a.m. because a horse race was scheduled for the afternoon. Despite the early hour and the blazing sun, crowds of people attended. Reinhard's estimate of those saved during the five days was seventy thousand.

He made a commitment then and there to hold other crusades in Ghana, which he has done. One was held in early 1986 at Kumasi, the second largest city, and in March 1986 at two smaller coastal towns. At the Kumasi crusade, a dozen blind people received their sight at one service. Day after day, the crusade was big news in Kumasi. Hardly a single person among the eight hundred thousand inhabitants was not aware that Jesus was visiting their city. Among those who took a keen interest was the king of the Ashantis, who was visited by Reinhard and the CFAN team.

The giant stadium at Kumasi, which seats eighty thousand people, had never been used for a Christian event before, and it overflowed with an estimated one hundred and twenty thousand people attending each service. Pastor Opuni of the Assemblies of God in Kumasi said, "A completely new and positive situation has arisen here. The spiritual climate has changed. We thank Jesus for this breakthrough."

The third major crusade in Ghana was held on a large open sports field half way between the towns of Sekondi and Takoradi. During the five days, crowds varied between sixty thousand and eighty thousand. Local ministers were amazed at the turnout. This was the first time a large-scale crusade had been held in the western region of Ghana. According to local pastor Eogre Appekey, general secretary of the Assemblies of God and chairman of the crusade committee, the previous largest crowd for a Christian event had been less than five thousand people.

Seven blind people received their sight. Among the cripples who walked that night was a twenty-year-old man who had been carried into the meeting. He jumped up and ran to the platform to tell what had happened. He had no shoes because he had never had to wear them! So Reinhard gave him the money to buy a new pair for his newly healed feet.

Reinhard wrote in the German edition of *Missions-Reportage:*

"The peak of the crusade was without doubt the moment when Jesus baptized thousands of new converts with the Holy Ghost and Fire. It was like Pentecost in the Book of Acts. The glory of the Lord came down like liquid fire. Many thousands received the gift of praising the Lord in a new language. The western region of Ghana will never be the same because these people, ignited by the Holy Spirit, will carry the fire everywhere. In Jesus' name, this will continue in country after country. We can rest one day in Heaven — but *now* is harvest time."

Easter in London

The trip to the United Kingdom was for the Easter Day service at the Royal Albert Hall. This famous London landmark was almost filled to capacity. According to locals, it was one of the largest religious gatherings since pre-World War II days. One elderly woman, who had been attending the Easter services there for the past fifty years, exclaimed, "It is the greatest meeting I have ever been to . . . I'll never be the same again."

As usual, Reinhard's anointed preaching generated a high level of faith and an urgency to get involved with promoting the Gospel. This was confirmed by a spokesman for Elim Bible College who said that the number of applicants to attend the college skyrocketed following his message, "Faith Frightens Satan."

In November 1985, Reinhard returned to England lighting further flames of revival. From the first meeting held in the Watford Town Hall, it was clear that accommodating the crowd was going to be the major problem. At the first meeting, some two hundred and fifty "home folks" volunteered to leave so that visitors could hear the preaching.

The next two meetings were held in Westminster Chapel, London, and that grand old building was filled to capacity. With uninhibited rejoicing, the crowd witnessed a young man, who had only walked on crutches for thirty years, take his first faltering steps holding onto the pews. Finally, he ran down the aisles and leaped onto the platform holding his crutches in the air!

A tightly packed schedule on this trip included meetings at the Central Hall, Birmingham; the Town Hall in Leeds; the large new Halton Pentecostal Church in Widnes, which seats fifteen hundred people; and the recently completed Leisure Centre in Newport, south Wales. Such was the response that at some meetings as many as five hundred people had to be turned away because of fire and safety rules governing crowd capacities. At Leeds, a man began pushing his own wheelchair up and down the aisles and stood worshiping the Lord for the remainder of the service.

Truly, the winds of the Holy Spirit are sweeping through Britain. Reports similar to this have been received from other evangelists who recently have been to the United Kingdom.

"Bonnke Shakes Perth"

In December 1985, Reinhard stopped over in Perth, Australia, accompanied by Pastor Ray McCauley of Rhema Ministries South Africa, for a two-day rally before continuing on to Singapore. The headlines of the daily newspaper, *The West Australian*, summed up the visit: "Bonnke Shakes Perth."

A total of twenty-three churches and local fellowships had combined to rent the Entertainment Centre where up to seven thousand attended each night with hundreds making first-time decisions for the Lord.

"Even though the crusade was so short, it was the best we have ever had in Perth," said local organiser, Pastor Brian Baker. "It is the first time that so many churches in this city have cooperated. That is a miracle in itself," he added.

On the second evening of the rally, an outstanding miracle not only shook up those people in the hall but made major headlines the following day. While preaching, Reinhard approached a woman sitting in a wheelchair and told her he had a Word from the Holy Spirit that she was to be healed during the service.

"Do you believe that?" asked Reinhard.

The woman's head slumped onto her chest. Her faith was too weak to give a positive reply.

It was an extremely bold moment, but earlier in the day Reinhard had been assured by the Holy Spirit that the Lord was going to heal a woman in a green sweater. When his eyes fell on the woman in the wheelchair, wearing a green top, he knew she was the one.

A wave of faith flowed through him, leaving a holy audacity that even surprised him. He took the woman by the hand and began to pray for her. Then with a hushed audience looking on, he told her to stand up in the name of Jesus. In that moment, it happened. The power of God shot into her limbs. She jumped out of the wheelchair totally healed. It was almost impossible to quieten the crowd who began rejoicing and praising God for this miracle. The woman had been told by doctors that she might never walk again, but God had done in one glorious moment what was impossible for man.

A Perth television crew was at the meeting and filmed this dramatic healing as it occurred. The incident was shown nationwide the following day. There also was a film clip showing Reinhard laughing and smiling as he was wheeled across the stage in the woman's wheelchair.

Visited the next day by local newspaper reporters, the healed woman opened the front door herself. "Her wheelchair stood folded in the hall," the papers reported. Pastor Baker followed up on this healing and later sent CFAN a letter with a doctor's report that indicated that initially Mrs. Shirley McKelt had broken the neck of the femur bone and was unable to walk. She had an operation two weeks prior to the meeting but had still been unable to walk. After the meeting, an X-ray showed new bone growth which normally should have taken at least ten weeks, the doctors said. Stiffness in muscles and nerves also had disappeared, and the doctors gave the thirty-four-year-old woman an "excellent report."

A Visit to Singapore

At first, Reinhard had been reluctant to become involved in a major crusade outside of Africa, but later he agreed. The magnificent, modern stadium in Singapore was booked for the 11th through the 15th of December. The Church there immediately shifted into high gear, and with typical Oriental precision and diligence planned every detail. Chris Lodewyk went over to assist. Because this was to be a full-blown CFAN operation, it was decided that Suzette Hattingh also should go on ahead and prepare the spiritual ground with her intercessory prayer groups.

A total of seven churches cooperated, with the large and influential Charismatic Anglican church headed by Bishop Dr. Moses Tai playing a major role in organizing and preparing for the crusade. Full-page newspaper advertisements were placed, and posters set up in most public places and on buses. Special t-shirts were made up for the event.

Singapore is a very unusual nation. Despite its lack of size and absence of natural resources — except the harbor and strategic location in east Asia — it is exceptionally prosperous. It is a small and crowded country of two and a half million people, consisting mainly of idol-worshipers, Moslems, and Christians. Those who worship idols make up by far the greater percentage and even the number of Moslems is about double that of Christians.

Despite being in the minority, Christians hold many high positions in business, commerce, and government circles. In fact, the Christians in Singapore are among the most affluent in the world. They have, thankfully, recognized that this temporal blessing is for the promotion of the Gospel. Singapore is not only a nation and city of many religions, but also of cultures and languages, making its success as a unitary state even more remarkable.

The Singapore crusade was a test for Reinhard. He explains, "From the very first night, I realized that there were many heathens in the stadium — people who had absolutely no Biblical knowledge. I was gripped by a deep urge to teach these dear people to know Jesus and His redemptive work on the cross. And God's grace was with us. The Holy Spirit revealed Jesus, and thousands of precious souls acknowledged Him as the Son of the Living God."

On the night Reinhard preached on the baptism of the Holy Spirit, thousands experienced the reality of this wonderful Bible promise. "Never before have we heard an entire stadium full of people singing in tongues," was the amazed comment of one Chinese organizer. An odd thing happened during that service. As Reinhard preached on the Holy Spirit, a large white bird suddenly flew into the middle of the stadium and hovered all the while within the arcs of the powerful floodlights. "It is a sign from God! The Holy Spirit is here," people whispered to each other in the stands. As cripples jumped out of wheelchairs and cancers disappeared, the comment was heard over and over, "This is a breakthrough for Singapore."

In addition to the nightly crusades, Reinhard was asked to speak to six hundred lecturers at the national university. The hall was overflowing with professors and instructors, representing many religions. Reinhard, never ashamed to present the truth and claims of Jesus boldly and clearly, preached from Mark 15 on the heathen centurion who stood at the foot of the cross and had a revelation that Jesus is the Son of the Living God. Afterwards, he invited them to accept Jesus, and a number of the learned men responded to the altar call.

During the five-day crusade, crowds of up to fifty thousand attended each service, and at least seven thousand decisions were made for Christ. The impact among the heathen community was great, and the Church in Singapore immediately asked Reinhard and the team to return for an even larger crusade in 1987. He also received invitations to hold crusades in Malaysia and the Philippine Islands, extending his vision not only to all of Africa but to answer a call from the East to **come over . . . and help us** (Acts 16:9) as well.

The United Charismatic Convention

Shortly after the Singapore meeting, Reinhard returned "Down Under" with his destination this time being the South Australian capital of Adelaide. There he shared the platform with Dr. Paul Yonggi Cho of South Korea, among others. The event was the annual United Charismatic Convention, organized by Barry Chant, who had invited Reinhard to attend when Chant first met him at the Big Tent dedication in February 1984.

As part of the convention and as an outreach to Adelaide, permission was obtained to hold an open-air meeting in Victoria Square — but it was limited to one hour. Reinhard was given the honor of preaching, and many came forward to accept Jesus. Overlooking Victoria Square is the Hilton Hotel where a Canadian businessman was staying. He heard the Gospel from his bedroom window and gave his life to Jesus as well. The man came and told Reinhard about his decision and joined the delegates at the conference for the rest of the week — another example of the power of the Gospel to reach into the heart of man, whether in a mass meeting or alone in a hotel bedroom in a foreign city.

15

RACISM CHALLENGED

The year 1985 must rank as the most traumatic of all the years of the ministry for Reinhard — and for the team. The Big Tent had been lost the year before, but that turned out to be mostly a financial blow and nothing to the upheaval that occurred in 1985. It seemed that in the midst of the greatest victories of the Bonnke ministry, everything that could be shaken was shaken.

First, there was the move into genuine mass evangelism and the crusades in Ibadan and Singapore; secondly, there was the tragic death of two of the crew following the Zambia and Zaire crusades; and, last of all, there came the momentous unexpected necessity to uproot the organization from South Africa. This latter situation caused the most serious upheaval of all for the ministry. Many of the CFAN team had to quit, and the move even caused some confusion for Christians in South Africa. Also, an international headquarters had to be found, property had to be bought and sold. All of these things amounted to an earthquake in many people's lives.

None of these events or decisions, however, were apparent when CFAN department heads met January 11, 1985, for a routine meeting. Some attention was given to finances and the need to budget wisely. Reinhard shared some of his plans for the future and warned of difficulties that would be encountered because of those plans of expanding the vision further into Africa: lower living standards, dangers of disease, and generally harsher conditions for the crusade team on the road. He expressed a strong desire for each man to improve in his area of expertise and to strive for greater efficiency.

Reinhard talked about his intention to build up the CFAN Village as a multiracial community and strongly advised that women and children remain at home while the men went north on crusades. There was even talk of securing a large plane which could ferry the men to and from the crusades, giving them adequate time off to be at home with their families. Members of the ministry left the meeting feeling their futures were reasonably secure. Little did they know what would transpire before they next met in eight weeks time. Christians need to place their security only in God. Things on earth are always changing. Only He does not change.

In addition to a series of international speaking engagements, Reinhard and Peter Vandenburg decided to spy out the land farther north in Africa. Shortly after that staff meeting, they toured six countries on the West Coast: Togo, the Ivory Coast, Nigeria, Cameroons, Ghana, and Upper Volta. They gained valuable information and established some vital new contacts, such as that with Archbishop Idahosa. The Ibadan crusade came out of this tour.

Perhaps the most important thing they found out, however — and the one which had the greatest impact on the ministry — was the discovery that CFAN's connections with South Africa were potentially a far greater hindrance than they had ever considered.

Reinhard, during his travels overseas and into Africa, had often faced a barrage of hostile questions from the media concerning South Africa. His answer always was that he regards himself as a preacher and part of the solution. Unfortunately, some of the antagonism and naked hatred expressed towards anything remotely connected with South Africa was forceably brought home to Reinhard and Peter during their West Africa reconnaissance.

In Lagos, for example, they were told that people threw back Gospel tracts if they saw the tracts had been printed in Pretoria. It also became apparent that there was no way the South African members of the team would be allowed to travel in Africa with their present passports. On his return to Witfield, Reinhard had to bluntly tell the staff that he had come to a realistic conclusion that, if they were to win Africa for Jesus, they could not stay in South Africa.

He announced immediate steps to downgrade the South African office and to register one in Harare, Zimbabwe. He warned the South African staff members that they would have to obtain other passports if they wanted to remain with CFAN.

Things began to move swiftly. Fortunately, CFAN had maintained an office in Harare since 1984. It was now already the main center for the planning of the massive FIRE conference to be held in the Sheraton Centre. Staff and equipment had been flowing between Witfield and Harare for some months, and a good circle of contacts had been established in the Zimbabwean capital.

A major concern, however, remained the South African members of the team. Reinhard reiterated time and again that they would have to obtain some other passport and that this would be the responsibility of the individuals concerned. At the March 20 staff meeting, he asked everyone to be open and honest with regard to their desire to move north. He added that CFAN would do its best to help find alternative employment for those who could not go, or did not want to go.

The number of key South African personnel at that time was considerable. For them, it became a mountainous problem. Initially, they did nothing. There were crusades to keep up with, and the ministry had to continue to function. Also, it was difficult to forecast when the move to Harare would be finalized.

By the end of April, it was announced that CFAN planned to buy a block of apartments in Harare, and by June this had been accomplished. Then it became obvious the move was going to come quicker than some people had expected. Some of the South African staff then began to make inquiries about immigrating to Zimbabwe in an attempt to legally get a new citizenship and passport.

To do this, they found, meant living in Zimbabwe for at least five years before qualifying for a passport. This, of course, was not feasible because the crusade team would constantly be on the move in Africa and because there was no guarantee that CFAN would be based in Zimbabwe for five years.

Now came an agonizing decision. Unless there was a miraculous change of heart, politically, about South Africa by its neighbors which would make their passports acceptable, all the South African staff members would have to leave the organization.

Some stoically reached that decision and began earnestly to seek the Lord and plan for the future. Some resigned during the second half of the year. Others chose to remain with the team for as long as possible, praying for a miracle or hoping the crusades would be confined for a time to those nations willing to accept South African passports.

Indeed, it was a trying time for everyone concerned. They had not only their own futures, but that of their children concerning schools and higher education, to consider.

The decision to downgrade the Witfield office and to establish Harare as the Africa base (for an unspecified time because it was apparent that the base eventually would have to move northwards) also forced another decision: to establish an international headquarters off the continent. Offices already had been set up in West Germany, the United States, and Great Britain. It was decided that international headquarters should be in Europe because of the possibility of flying easily to most of the capitals of Africa from Europe. For obvious reasons, Reinhard voted for Germany, and so a search began for a suitable base in West Germany.

Nine Glorious Days

In the meantime, the crusades and meetings continued from South Africa to Australia. One poignant meeting — especially under the circumstances of the decision to move — was the one held from April 27 to May 5 at the Pilditch sports arena in Pretoria, South Africa.

The city has heavy symbolic connotations. Militant international organizations scathingly refer to the

"Pretoria racist regime." In a sense, the city is seen as the bastion of Afrikanerdom (white Dutch-speaking natives) and the unjust system of apartheid. Just as Johannesburg is the commercial and financial pulse of South Africa, so Pretoria throbs out political signals.

Most of the world's news media and politicians have focused their attention in recent years on the creeping violence in South Africa, on disinvestment and sanctions, and the merry-go-round of proposed internal changes and reforms. What is overlooked is that most South Africans, of all races, have a deep desire for peace, harmony, and prosperity for the future.

Those words may sound hollow in view of the killings, arson, unemployment, and economic hazards which threaten the country. The plea of the nation is for solutions, but politicians, academicians, industrialists, clerics, and the news media churn out verbiage that is at best a desperate cry for help and, at worst, only exacerbates the already raw situation.

Racism undoubtedly is the ugly scar on the heart of South Africa, but at Pilditch sports arena, there was a demonstration of what God's love can do and is doing in this beleaguered nation. Much of the world's media ignore the good and concentrate on the bad and ugly. For nine days in 1985, the people of Pretoria — mainly Afrikaners — experienced something beautiful.

For nine days, blacks, whites, coloreds, and Indians filed into the Pilditch sports arena. They sang together, prayed together, wept together, and rejoiced together. For the thousands of whites who came, it was not only a meeting with God but a social education. Afrikaans-speaking citizens rubbed shoulders, held hands, and united in an unprecedented way with their black and brown brethren. They found that, under the skins of these Christians, were people who loved and served God as fervently as they did.

More than eighty thousand people attended the crusade with about sixteen thousand at the final Sunday afternoon meeting. Ministers were unanimous about the spirit of unity that prevailed. The ugliness of racism disappeared for nine glorious days.

Why? The answer is childishly simple: Jesus, the Man Who walked the dusty roads of Palestine nearly two thousand years ago is declared to be the *Prince of Peace*. His peace was powerfully demonstrated at the "Jesus '85 Crusade" in Pretoria. There on the grassy island of the sports field, the Gospel of reconciliation was demonstrated. Masks fell, and those Christians, black and white, who attended began to see that actually there are only two "races" to God — sinners and saints, or the saved and the unsaved. They began to see that they were all sinners once, no better and no worse than one another, whether they lived in a slum or a posh suburb. All of them needed the love of God and His salvation.

The Christians recognized another truth: they were all born of the same divine Spirit and forgiven as a result of the same divine sacrifice — Jesus. They found there was more to agree about than to disagree about. Nightly they came to sing, worship, and to lift up holy hands to the Lord. Nightly, they prayed together for a single purpose: to see the Kingdom of God enlarged. Nightly, they rejoiced to see hundreds of sinners turn to the Lord in repentance and find new life, hope, and peace in Jesus.

One of the CFAN team was part of a small prayer group one night which consisted of a black man, an Afrikaans-speaking white man, and an English-speaking white man. He noted the symbolism of the threesome and thanked God for it. He said, "For only in Jesus is there true reconciliation and harmony."

But what did the Pretoria crusade demonstrate to South Africa, sick with prejudice and weeping because of the human damage caused by apartheid? Simply this: if South Africa is truly a Christian nation, then it needs to turn Godward for its solutions. The Christianity of the nation has consisted of a large part of lip service; its past style of Christianity has been stained with the bile of racism, and the time has now come for all white leaders to hear and do the Word of God.

To reject the way of peace — God's way — offered by practical Christianity will bring South Africa into perilous and dark times. The answers for all of mankind were encapsulated in that Pretoria crusade. It was a different crusade. It lacked the spontaneity of Ibadan, the zest of Harare, but it was characterized by waves of divine love that reached down into the depths of every heart.

This great victory for love and unity was forged by long and arduous planning by the Pretoria crusade committee, on which men like Pastor Willie Crew labored with a large and enthusiastic team of volunteers who worked for months to ensure that the event would proceed smoothly.

Also, there was the spiritual preparation and warfare, spearheaded as usual by Suzette Hattingh. Few of the city's population knew anything about this part of the crusade. The invisible battle was fought by a hardy band of five hundred intercessory prayer warriors, who raised their voices to Heaven and released the power of God over the city.

Suzette relates, "When I arrived in Pretoria to prepare the intercessory prayer squads, I immediately sensed a strong spiritual resistance."

Realizing that they were in for a real battle, she soon got rid of the slackness in the volunteers' prayer lives. "I knew they had to be taught how to make war and that God was raising up an army for Himself," she added.

From then on, it was all-out warfare in the spirit realm as from three hundred to five hundred people of all races gathered to listen to the Word and to intercede.

"It was the highest level of unity in spiritual warfare that I have experienced in our crusades," she says, "Not only were we interceding for the meetings but for the city as well. People began to stand in authority and pray with a deep assurance that their prayers were turning back the enemy. The intercessors knew they were engaged in real spiritual combat."

Suzette directs her intercessors as a general would his troops. On the final Saturday night and Sunday afternoon of the crusade, she changed strategies. Instead of remaining in a hall at the back of the stadium, the intercessors moved in among the crowd.

"We had people under the platform praying all the time, and others ringed the front of the platform. We built up a 'wall' of prayer. Still other groups were in the grandstand," she says.

The impact of her prayer ministry not only produces glorious results during the CFAN crusades but has a profound effect on the volunteers who join her army temporarily. They rarely remain the same, but they return to their churches on fire and thrilled to have gotten to grips with the reality of prayer. Many pastors have been inspired by the often revolutionary-to-them approach to prayer. In the beginning, some pastors regarded the intercessory groups as "just another prayer meeting." But this attitude soon changed once they became absorbed in the teaching and practice of genuine intercession.

In addition to the love and joy that marked this crusade, there were some heartwarming testimonies of healing, but the greatest joy of all came from the fifty-three hundred new converts who were closely followed up by the dozens of churches that cooperated in a meeting that stands out in a year of outstanding crusades.

A Strain on Resources

In November, Reinhard was in Frankfurt and, while there, saw a property that looked good for a headquarters site. It had good grounds, offices, and several apartments. It was near the city and, of vital importance, close to the international airport. The price also seemed good. The property was being sold by a bank that had seized it after the owners had gone bankrupt.

He made an offer and took an option on the property. At a meeting back in Witfield where he asked the team to pray about the property, he confidently predicted that CFAN would clinch the deal at a good price. A few weeks later, CFAN had its international headquarters.

In the meantime, the move to Harare had been in full swing since the middle of 1985. Estimates were that the vehicle fleet would have to take thirty-five loads of equipment. Staff began moving into the Harare apartments where momentum was gathering for the For Inter-African Revival Evangelists Conference, now set for April 1986, and for the Big Tent crusade which was to run in conjunction with the international conference.

Those three factors — the moving job, the conference, and crusade preparation — put an unbelievable strain on CFAN's limited human and financial resources. At the same time, expansion was occurring with the purchase of the Frankfurt base and also the establishment of a West African base. As the changes began to develop, a strategy began to emerge. The new Big Tent, to be ready and in action by conference time, would concentrate on crusades in southern and central Africa, while a mobile team operated from a base in Nigeria, organizing open-air meetings there and in neighboring countries.

The West African base was to be established by a seasoned and astute CFAN staff member and his wife, Winfried and Gabi Wentland. He was to have a complete sound system, a platform, lights, and a truck, and he would be in charge of all the technical arrangements for all the West African Crusades.

From Harare, plans were to reach into Malawi, Tanzania, Uganda, and Kenya with the Big Tent. The move into Africa was no longer talk. It was happening and much faster than anyone had anticipated. For example, at one point Reinhard had hoped the final move out of South Africa would be completed by the end of 1986. Actually, the Witfield complex closed officially on May 31!

Most of the South African staff had come to a final decision by that time. Looking back on that traumatic time, it appears that — as hard as the changes were to many people — most of the upheaval has been beneficial to the Kingdom of God. CFAN, like all dynamic ministries, attracted a number of people who develop and mature greatly from their experiences with an evangelist such as Reinhard. Eventually, however, the time comes when the "eaglets" have to leave the nest and fly by themselves. That apparently is what God accomplished through all the shaking that went on. Letting go of the ministry was one of the hardest hurdles for some to cross. A number of them, however, are now in Bible school or in ministries of their own.

The scaling down of the operation in South Africa unfortunately was misinterpreted by some white Christians as running away from trouble and unrest. Many thought Reinhard should remain and continue to preach there in an effort to bring about a change of heart that will stop the violence. His priority, however, has never been South Africa. His calling always has been to Africa as a whole, and South Africa was only a small part of that vision. There is an entire continent to be reached, and Reinhard was not prepared to jeopardize his commission and calling for the sake of any political ideology.

He steers clear of political storms, although he is vehemently opposed to apartheid. He has never used the pulpit to pontificate to political leaders, whether left, right, or center. His message centers on Jesus, the only true way of peace and reconciliation. Reinhard says he is willing to preach in the capital of the "racist Pretoria regime," in Moscow's Red Square, or in the citadel of democracy and capitalism, Washington, D.C.

CFAN, however, will maintain a small office in South Africa to handle correspondence and distribute video and audio tapes and maintain a link with the thousands of faithful prayer partners there who share the vision to see Africa won for Jesus. That will be the office's only function. All of the central administration will be controlled from Frankfurt with close cooperation with the regional offices in West Africa and Zimbabwe, or later in Nairobi.

By the end of 1986, the last of the South African passport holders left the team, and Reinhard's links with the "deep south" were almost all severed. Fortunately, a large number of the South African prayer partners do appreciate the expediency of CFAN's move and will continue to pray and support the ministry, even at long distance.

To Sell or Not to Sell

An immediate question that arose when the move from South Africa was first mooted was what would become of the Witfield complex? What at first may have seemed a simple question turned into a controversial issue with many people shaking their heads in bewilderment. The decisions involved caused some people to wonder what the Lord's will really was in the matter, because the decision was first to sell, then to give it away, but in the end to sell.

In June, Reinhard intended to sell the property as soon as possible. After spending some time in fellowship one weekend in late July with other ministers in Durban, he returned to the office believing he was to give the property away — a $500,000 gift. A letter went to all CFAN prayer partners outlining crusade plans and sharing his vision for the future of Witfield:

"We have received a very clear word from God to move our main base to Europe where we will be able to reach the countries in question with greater ease. Our base at Witfield will be closed. I had intended selling it so as to be in a position to purchase a replacement overseas, but the Lord clearly spoke to me that I should not do so. This base will become a center for intercession and fasting, so that 'the angel of death' will be stopped in Africa. We have taken this decision in obedience to the Word of the Lord. To take this step is not easy, because we desperately need the money to establish a new base. I am throwing myself, with my team, into the arms of the Lord. He will see us through. Please pray for us."

His decision was met with many a gasp. It was certainly a magnanimous gesture, and some of the staff rejoiced. Others believed the property should still be sold. To Christians outside the ministry, it was a breathtaking decision and greatly admired. The big question which now arose — and the one which may have resulted in the decision being changed — was: Who was to get the property?

Reinhard wanted it to go to a ministry that had a vision for Africa to be saved. He had expressed the hope that it would become a center for prayer, fasting, teaching, and intercession — a hub for many facets of evangelism and missions — with a view to unity for all in Africa. He added, however, that he was prepared to turn over the property with no strings attached, except that the facility become a point of unity to reach the rest of Africa.

The word soon spread throughout the country and telephone calls and letters began to come in from many ministries and individuals. Almost everyone of them believed, emphatically, that the Lord had given *them* a word for the property! The months drifted by and no decision was reached. One or two people put forward plans to make use of the complex, but it became apparent that there was no ministry with the financial muscle and size capable of making full use of the property.

Schemes for several ministries sharing the complex were put forward, but none of them seemed really workable. Then somebody remarked that Witfield would become an "ecclesiastical refugee camp." It seemed that the apparently simple thing of giving away the property was, in fact, mined with problems. Reinhard found himself in a position where his gift had become an offense. Clearly by giving it to one person or group, he was going to hurt others who felt they should have received it.

He wrestled with the puzzle. First he had wanted to sell it, then he was sure the Lord said give it away. Now the saints were squabbling over the gift! One thing for sure, the Lord is never happy about strife and contention in the Body. And too many people had gotten into the soulish realm over this thing, so possibly the "little foxes" had spoiled the vine. (Song of Sol. 2:15.) Finally, in February 1986, a pastor colleague, Ed Roebert of Pretoria — regarded as a man of high integrity and one who knows the voice of the Lord — gave him a green light confirming that he was to take back his "gift" and sell the property.

The scriptural backing for the reversal of the decision was Abraham's placing of Isaac on the altar and being given his "sacrifice" back. The Witfield complex had been Reinhard's "Isaac." He had laid it on the altar, and now God was allowing him to pick it up again and sell it. The change of decision once again rocked many people, of course, who began to doubt whether he really had heard from the Lord.

The next step, however, was to contact the ministries that had shown an interest and ask them if they wanted to buy. There were no takers, however. The next step was to advertise in the secular press. Then contact was made with Jan de Rouwe, a wealthy businessman, who is also senior pastor of the East Rand Christian Centre and a long-time supporter of CFAN. His desire for many years had been to start a Christian school. The complex would suit his purpose ideally. After several weeks of negotiations, the sale was finalized during the FIRE conference at Harare. The Witfield office complex and Reinhard's own home were sold as a block to de Rouwe. Another phase of his ministry had come to an end: first Germany, then the first African phase uprooted them to Johannesburg, now the second African phase was moving them from Johannesburg into a truly international ministry. Only the Lord knows if there will be further moves.

16
FIRE ACROSS AFRICA

In the last days, God says, I will pour out My Spirit on all people . . . . I will show wonders in the heaven above and signs on the earth below. . . . And everyone who calls on the name of the Lord will be saved.

Acts 2:17, 19, 21 NIV

When the all-Africa conference on evangelism was first mentioned by Reinhard, the number of delegates was estimated at six hundred or seven hundred. The event initially was to have been held in Swaziland. Later, the location was switched to Harare, Zimbabwe, and the dates also were changed. At first, it was to be late 1984, then 1985, and finally, April 1986. By then the scope of the conference had become truly international.

The actual number of delegates amounted to four thousand, with nearly a fourth of them sponsored. Some of the world's finest speakers were invited to the conference, For Inter-African Revival Evangelists (FIRE) of the Holy Spirit.

When Reinhard first got the idea for the conference, he had no one on staff who could organize such an event. There was talk of hiring an outside agency, but as so often happens, he did not let the "finer details" of the project bother him. If God had ordained the event, then He would provide the wherewithal, including personnel and finances — and He did.

As mentioned earlier, one of the things that God did in the midst of the Big Tent destruction in Cape

Town was to introduce Chris Lodewyk to CFAN, and it was upon him that the responsibility for organizing the FIRE conference fell. It proved to be his toughest assignment to date. Probably there are few professional conference planners who would have attempted the task with a small staff, restricted budget, and CFAN's lack of experience in an international event. The things Lodewyk did in getting the staff geared up for the event and in handling multiple complications was often amazing.

It is hard for Westerners to appreciate the difficulties encountered in organizing events in Africa. Fortunately, CFAN has gained this experience from its crusade planning, and Chris was forewarned about some of the obstacles he would encounter. One major difficulty is communications. Telephones are apt to go out of order regularly. Telexes are not very plentiful. Mail delivery service also is unreliable. So obstacle number one was the communications problem.

Obstacle number two was the poverty of much of Africa, meaning that most of the delegates would not be able to pay their own way, or at least not all of it. This immediately raised the third obstacle: Who would be chosen to attend? There was no lack of preachers wanting to be sponsored, but how to pick those who were not just conference "hoppers" or those who had a real calling and vision in their ministries?

This meant trying to establish contact with reputable men of God in each nation of Africa, and this was no easy job. Open-minded men of integrity had to be found, men who had a vision for the Kingdom of God, and not those interested only in building up their own empires. The contacts had to be men with a vision for their nation and for Africa.

To find these contacts meant sending men into Africa to travel extensively and spy out the land. Among these were Werner Drotleff and Ekkehard Homburg, both of CFAN, and Mike Oman, Youth With a Mission director in Zimbabwe. Then thousands of applications were taken. After that came the long, drawn-out process of examining each one and checking out references, which took months and months because of obstacle number one: communications.

Obstacle number four was transportation. Once the delegates were selected, the next step was to coordinate their travel to Harare. Many were able to come by road from neighboring countries such as Mozambique, Malawi, Zambia, Zaire, Lesotho, Swaziland, Botswana, and South Africa. But, for those farther north, travel meant getting an airplane flight, and this is easier said than done.

Most African nations have their own internal flights, but international flights are mainly confined to the major airlines operating from Europe. At one point, it looked as if some delegates would have to fly to London and then back to Harare! In the end, many delegates had to catch at least four connecting flights to attend the conference. To assist with this, CFAN chartered several flights. One went to Lagos, which became a central meeting place on the West Coast; another flew to Nairobi on the East Coast.

Even then, unforeseen things happened. The Lagos charter was impounded by airport officials because certain fees had not been paid. Fortunately, Mike Oman had accompanied the flight to Lagos and after making representation to some of the highest authorities, including the chief of the air force, the matter was resolved. The fees *had* been paid, but someone had "put their hand in the till." Corruption among officialdom, unfortunately, is a way of life in many parts of Africa.

Then there were immigration and customs problems. Applications for visas and the importing of goods and equipment for the running of the conference had to be approved by the various governments involved. Key personnel who worked closely with Lodewyk in this area were Americans Bud and Doris Horton, who had given up their own business in the United States to join CFAN. Another vital link was Zimbabwean Chris Alberts who had the heavy responsibility of negotiating with customs and immigration authorities.

All members of CFAN, of course, were engaged in certain areas of the conference, and volunteers in the Harare area helped immensely. Then came the obstacle of accommodations. Some twenty-two hotels were booked, while hundreds of Christians opened their homes to those who could not afford to pay for hotels. All of this had to be financed, and a real miracle of finances needed to be achieved.

Reinhard admits that even in January before the event, he almost postponed the conference again because response had been lukewarm and finances were low. Funds were exceptionally tight because of his continuing commitment to crusades combined with the moving of bases around the world. In mid-January, he and Peter met with Chris and discussed the problems. Then "the Spirit of God came on me and a soothing peace flooded me," recalls Reinhard. Chris told him he urgently needed $400,000. Reinhard promised he would get it to him within a week — and he did. God provided!

From an organizational aspect, the conference was a huge success. So much so that the Zimbabwean government asked Chris to assist them on certain aspects of a forthcoming conference of non-aligned states. The greatest success of the conference, however, was spiritual.

Speakers represented various flows and ministries within the Kingdom of God. Included were Loren Cunningham, founder of Youth With a Mission; Kenneth and Gloria Copeland, Bible teachers of Fort Worth, Texas; Wayne Myers from Mexico; Ralph Mahoney, founder of World Mission Assistance Plan; Bishop Benson Idahosa from Nigera; Dr. Ron Shaw from Mark Buntain's mission in India; Dr. Robert Schuller of California; and, from South Africa, Ray McCauley, Elijah Maswanganyi, Ed Roebert, and Nicky van der Westhuizen. Of course, Reinhard spoke, as did Suzette Hattingh from CFAN.

The theme of the conference was every aspect of evangelism, and these gifted speakers made a valuable and lasting contribution to the vision and commission for the salvation of Africa. Forty-one African nations, including some of the Indian Ocean islands, were represented. Also there were visitors from America, Great Britain, West Germany, Norway, Sweden, Denmark, France, Singapore, and Australia.

From the outset, Reinhard stated that the prime reason for the conference was to set aflame a spark in the hearts of God's servants that each would go back to his or her village, town, or city and help set the nations alight for Jesus.

The hearts of all who attended were stirred by the visibly demonstrated unity within the Body of Christ. Reinhard has never shown partiality toward any denomination, and this had not been a consideration in screening applications. So men and women from a variety of denominations and ministries found themselves together in Harare. The Holy Spirit did a glorious job of welding them together and showing them the folly of artificial barriers, which divided.

If unity was a force at work, so too was evangelism. Speakers challenged delegates time and again to widen their vision and their expectations. An urgent message of the conference was to accept the challenge to change nations by the power of the Gospel.

Since the conference, hundreds of letters have poured into the CFAN offices telling of the fires lit in the hearts of hundreds of delegates and of their determination to put into practice what they learned and saw at the conference. When the event came to a close, there were many requests for a future conference of the same nature.

A special and very different feature of this conference was the crusade being held in conjunction with it. Nightly, delegates were able to go to the new Big Tent to see mass evangelism in action. For many it was a new dimension of ministry to see thousands responding to altar calls and to see the power of God demonstrated when the sick were prayed for and healed.

Many left saying, "I'll never be the same again." The FIRE Conference was indeed a life-changing experience, even for Reinhard himself. He spoke at the opening ceremony and gave the final address on the closing Saturday morning. That service will never be forgotten by anyone who was there. In the opulent conference center with the flags of fifty nations bedecking the balconies, the Holy Spirit moved in a powerful and mighty way that saw Reinhard crumple to the floor under the anointing of the Spirit. Guest speakers surrounded and prayed for him, and American evangelist Dave Newberry brought a powerful prophecy that thundered through the center.

The central theme of the prophecy was that a greater outpouring of God's Spirit is coming and that Reinhard would, in the name of Jesus, "subdue nations" and stand before "kings and rulers." The prophecy added that the Lord was gathering a "mighty army" that would undergird the CFAN ministry. This was, indeed, the "hour of a new move of the Holy Spirit in the world."

The closing ceremony of the conference was a communion service held in the Big Tent on Sunday morning. It was a touching service with close to twenty thousand Christians sharing the bread and wine and remembering their mighty Savior.

The guest speakers also left Harare deeply touched by what God is doing in Africa. They all sensed that the conference was, indeed, the beginning of a great outpouring of the Holy Spirit upon the continent.

Kenneth Copeland was ecstatic about what he had seen and said, "We are approaching God's finest hour. We are seeing the salvation of a continent. I have seen things at the FIRE conference which I have never experienced before. The atmosphere was charged with revival, faith, and a unity that thrilled my heart. In fact, it is the greatest spirit of revival that I have ever seen."

Loren Cunningham added, "The first night when I heard Brother Bonnke declare *'Africa shall be saved,'* I was excited, because I did not just hear the voice of a man but the very heart cry of God. 'Africa shall be saved' is a statement of faith. The fire of God is touching lives especially in the area of evangelism and healing."

That theme was echoed by Bishop Benson Idahosa, a long-time campaigner in Africa, who said, "This was a God-ordained event to lift us up. Our previous maximums became our minimums, and we now look for greater things to happen. 'Africa shall be saved' is not a slogan. No, it is a reality. Men of God across the continent are going to begin to take united action to save Africa . . . evangelist Bonnke is a precious gift . . . a treasure to the people of Africa. I urge Christians to back him up with their prayers and support."

The conference was a fulfillment of the divine dream deposited in Reinhard's heart in late 1983 and a vindication of his faith and vision during the times when the conference seemed doomed because of lack of finances or the immense logistical and political difficulties involved in its organization. Those intimately involved in the long build-up to the event knew that it was truly brought about by divine grace.

Reinhard summed up the conference like this, "In the nineteen years of evangelizing in Africa, I have never experienced such a mighty release of new gifts and anointings of the Holy Spirit. I believe we have reached a major turning point in Africa. I have always preached and believed that Africa shall be saved and this conference was a tangible step towards achieving the divine goal."

A lot of the spiritual effects of the conference can be attributed to the accompanying crusade meetings held in the new Big Tent. This gave delegates first-hand examples of mass evanglism and of praying for the sick. One delegate said it was like years of training all wrapped up in one week. The crusade attracted thousands every night, and there were eight thousand six hundred first-time decisions for Christ recorded. There also were multiple healings.

The fact that the crusade was held at all was a direct answer to prayer in which Suzette Hattingh and her diligent team of intercessors played a large part. From the beginning of the organizing of the event, it had been planned to run the conference and the crusade side by side despite the heavy burden it represented to CFAN's limited resources. Once the conference center had been booked, the next step had been to find a crusade site fairly close.

When the site was found and permission granted by the Harare City Council, the technical team immediately went to work. This was to be the first erection of the new tent, designed by a British firm and constructed in West Germany. Although the original basic design was maintained, there were certain alterations, and it was vital that the technical crew get a change to do some tests before the crusade began.

In the meantime, some residents who lived near the open fields where the tent was to be raised began to raise objections — especially when they saw the size of the tent. They were concerned about the influx of thousands of people and the attendant traffic into their area. There began a long series of objections which eventually led to a High Court injunction. The Harare

City Council stuck to their guns, however, with CFAN giving assurances about noise and crowd control.

The court action dragged on and the final judgment in favor of CFAN came only days before the crusade was to begin. Another attempt by Satan to halt the Gospel had been defeated. Again, however, it had been a battle waged more in the spirit world than in the natural with prayer intercessors in the frontline.

The New Big Tent

When the Big Tent fabric was destroyed in Cape Town in May 1984, as mentioned earlier, it was soon discovered that optimistic hopes for a quick insurance settlement were doomed. The claim became bogged down in a series of technicalities. It became apparent that full payment might be in doubt and, even if so, it would be a long process to settle. In the meantime, Reinhard was pushing to get a new roof — but how to raise the money?

He confided in his close South African friend, Ray McCauley, about his concern for a new roof. McCauley studied at Dr. Kenneth Hagin's Rhema Bible Training Center in Tulsa, Oklahoma, before returning to South Africa to begin Rhema Ministries there. Ray promised to help anyway he could. The two men soon flew to America on a brief speaking engagement, and it was during this visit that God provided the money to pay for a new tent roof.

Reinhard and Ray paid a visit to Kenneth Copeland's ministry headquarters in Fort Worth, Texas, as part of their American tour. As the three men shared together over breakfast in a city restaurant, the Spirit of God suddenly intervened in the discussion.

Reinhard and Ray stopped talking. Across the table, Copeland spoke out boldly, obviously under a powerful anointing of the Holy Spirit. What he said caused Reinhard's eyes to open wide in amazement.

"I'll pay for a new tent roof," were the words that came out of Copeland's mouth, but because of the anointing, they could have come directly from the throne room of the Almighty.

The atmosphere vibrated with a holy urgency and the plates of bacon and eggs looked as out of place to the three men as their "hallelujahs" did to their fellow diners. But God had spoken, and that was all that mattered. A new tent roof was on the way, and Reinhard could hardly wait to get back to his beloved continent of Africa. As the three men walked back out into the bright Texas sunlight, Reinhard's eyes blazed with an ardent zeal. Indeed, Africa would be saved! The devil would never halt the holy crusade through the continent.

Unknown to Reinhard at the time, however, was the fact that Kenneth Copeland Ministries was far from flush with money. Speaking at the new Big Tent dedication in Harare, Copeland shared with the congregation what a giant step of faith it had been for him to promise to pay for the roof.

His ministry, he said, was almost a million dollars behind in payments. But he had asked the Lord for a good place in which to sow seed for the finances he needed, and when he met with Reinhard over breakfast, the Holy Spirit had dropped into his heart that this was the place.

Believing beyond a doubt that this was the Lord's guidance, he had promised to pay the $800,000 needed for the replacement tent roof. When he told this story to the large audience under that roof in Harare, Copeland emphasized that, indeed, Jesus had paid for it.

"I never paid for it. Jesus paid for it," he said, and as he gave the glory to God, the thousands listening erupted into a wave of praise and thanksgiving.

Because of small structural changes, the profile of the new tent is more rounded and the interior space decreased slightly, although it will still seat close to thirty thousand people. With the experiences gained in the open-air crusades in West Africa and with the new move of the Holy Spirit, it is more than likely, however, that future Big Tent crusades will be standing room only. By eliminating the benches, it would be possible to get close to seventy thousand people under cover.

Some people still wonder why a tent is needed, especially as Reinhard has enjoyed such large and spectacular success in open-air meetings since 1984.

Not all city authorities will grant permission for open-air meetings, however. They claim the meetings are security risks. Also, sometimes it is not possible to obtain the use of stadiums. Then, of course, there is the weather. Heat or rain can make outdoor meetings very difficult, while the Big Tent provides good shelter from the elements for the majority of people attending most of the meetings.

Reinhard's African strategy is based now on a two-pronged attack: one is by means of outdoor meetings on the West Coast, and the other along the East Coast, is to use the Big Tent.

Already a base has been established in Ghana on the West Coast with a mobile team and a good sound system. Reinhard has always insisted on excellent sound equipment. "What is the good of people coming to a meeting if they cannot hear the message?" is his simple and obvious argument. In a June 1985 meeting when discussion centered on the West Coast sound system, it was explained to Reinhard that the present system had the capacity to reach four hundred thousand people.

He was not impressed. Looking across the room at the rest of the staff, he said, "That may be too small. *I have had a glimpse of the crowd that no man can number!*"

So instructions were given for a sound system that was capable of reaching a crowd of one million people!

It is difficult for Christians in Great Britain and America to appreciate just how open the people of Africa are for the Gospel, so that sound system may sound presumptuous to Westerners. But Africans are not just open. They are desperately hungry and are readily accepting Christ by the thousands. It is completely possible that millions will be accepting Him in the near future.

The real problem is how to cope with the mighty harvest. There is an acute shortage of well-trained pastors, and this is where other ministries are needed — to follow up behind Reinhard and his team. Also, despite the great harvesting opportunities, the obstacles are still great and sometimes dangerous. In addition to the besetting scourge of poverty with its attendant famine, Africa is a political melting pot. The very ingredients of poverty and hunger make the position of national leaders extremely precarious.

The forces of Islam and the insidious agents of Marxism are also at work on the African continent, where the multitudes of people and resources make the stakes high. Various ideologies are competing for the minds of the masses. For those with spiritual discernment, however, Africa is simply a giant chessboard with the nations as pawns between the players — the devil and the Church.

The Church has sometimes woefully failed in Africa, but God has raised up a man in Reinhard Bonnke, who will proclaim "Africa shall be saved" and then work to see it come to pass — not by feeding programs, not by foreign aid programs, not by politicians, not by capitalism or communism, but simply by the blood of Jesus Christ.

To fulfill the vision God has given him requires giant leaps of faith, where most Christians use tip-toe faith. The Big Tent was a giant leap of faith and so was the FIRE conference. The present all-out thrust into Africa is another giant leap of faith. The move to center his headquarters in Frankfurt is still another.

Although his calling and vision is for Africa, God perhaps has placed him in Europe for more than simple logistical reasons. Already, he is planning various conferences and campaigns for Europe. CFAN staff members and those people who have closely observed Reinhard's ministry, however, will not be surprised to one day see the Big Tent in Europe as well as in Cairo!

The harvest in Africa is ripe, and Reinhard and his team are reaping with an ardent fury. It may well be that the people of Africa who are eagerly embracing Christ as Savior may become the very evangelists to invade Europe in the next decade!

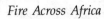

One thing is certain: Reinhard Bonnke will never turn his back on Africa. God called him to this great continent as a little boy, and his heart's desire remains to fulfill that sacred trust and to see his often-repeated statement come true:

Africa *shall* be saved!

DATE DE RETOUR